WHAT IS IN A NAME?

WHAT IS IN A NAME?

AN INQUIRY INTO THE SEMANTICS AND PRAGMATICS OF PROPER NAMES

by

FARHANG ZABEEH

Professor of Philosophy at Roosevelt University

MARTINUS NIJHOFF / THE HAGUE / 1968

ISBN 978-94-015-0452-2   ISBN 978-94-015-1094-3 (eBook)
DOI 10.1007/978-94-015-1094-3

Library of Congress Catalog Card Number: 68 – 25969

"What's in a name?"
Asked the poet.
"Everything",
Said the magician.
"Beware!
Thou shalt not take
The Lord's name
In vain."

"Nothing",
Said the logician.
"Change its sound and
You will change the name."

"Something",
Said Socrates.
"For see
What happened to me
When
The Pythian prophetess
Hung 'the wisest' on
My name."

F. Z.

CONTENTS

I. PRELIMINARIES

Poets, magicians, linguists, and logicians have often been fascinated, puzzled and angered by the protean functions of proper names. The interest of poets was mostly concerned with the connotations which the phonemes and the morphemes of personal or place-names carry with themselves and may awaken the memory of syndry bits of information about the bearers of the names. Even a bare mentioning, a mere echo of the name of some significant person or place – not to speak of the significant use of such a name – may occasion the floating of forgotten images. As if the name which supposes to be a mere label for a thing tries to tell us that it can do many other things besides its supposed proper role – it can tell us tall tales about its bearer.

These multifarious functions of proper names are not as felicitous as some writers have imagined. Proust, for one, was fascinated by the fecundity of names. For he looks at names not simply as a bare label arbitrarily bestowed upon infants or boulevards or tattooed on skins, as they may be – in order that one determines unequivocally the identity of referents – but also as something real and substantial on *a par* with the bearers of the names.

"I thought of names," he writes, "not as an inaccessible ideal but as a real and enveloping substance into which I was about to plunge, the life not yet lived, the life intact and pure which I enclosed in them, gave to the most material pleasures, to the simplest scenes, the same attraction that they have in the works of the Primitives." [1]

Proust sees a vast difference between words which are common nouns, and hence to him are abstract, dead and opaque, and

---

[1] *Remembrance of Things Past*, "Place-Names: The Name," Moncriefe Translation, p. 298.

proper names which being the names of particular persons and places mirror their referents, albeit without a clear contour.

"Words present to us little pictures of things, lucid and normal, like the pictures that are hung on the walls of schoolrooms to give children an illustration of what is meant by a carpenter's bench, a bird, and an ant-hill; things chosen as typical of everything else of the same sort," he writes. "But names present to us – of persons and of towns which they accustom us to regard as individual, as unique, like persons – a confused picture, which draws from the names, from the brightness or darkness of their sound, the colour in which it is uniformly painted, like one of those posters, entirely blue or entirely red, in which, on account of the limitations imposed by the process used in their reproduction, or by the whim on the designer's part, are blue or red not only the sky and the sea, but the ships and the church and the people in the streets."

Proust, thus, is dead to the words which present to him a picture "typical as everything else of the same sort." What denotes a Lockean *abstract general idea* or a Galtonian composite photograph, i.e., a generic representation of nothing in particular but of something in general, evokes no emotion in him. But, let a familiar name of a place or of a person be mentioned, it opens to him stores of dreams. "The name of Parma, one of the towns that I most longed to visit, after reading the *Chartreuse*," he continues, "seeming to me compact and glossy, violet-tinted, soft, if anyone were to speak of such or such a house in Parma, in which I should be loged, he would give me the pleasure of thinking that I was to inhabit a dwelling that was compact and glossy, violet-tinted, soft, and that bore no relation to the houses in any other town in Italy, since I could imagine it only by the aid of that heavy syllable of the name Parma, in which no breath of air stirred, and all that I had made it assume of Stendhalian sweetness and the reflected hue of violets. And when I thought of Florence, it was of a town miraculously embalmed, ... As for Ballbec, it was one of those names ..." [1]

Is it not, one wonders, alarming to mix up the "resonance of the syllables" of a placename with "the stone and mortar" of that place or the charming name of "Maréchale de Guermantes," with that not so charming character? Perhaps, but so much more enchanting.

[1] *Ibid.*, p. 296.

Yet that which nurtures joy, may too foster sorrow. Shakespeare makes use of the manysidedness of names, i.e., the dual functions of personal names (label-connotation) to create a tragedy. In the *Tragedy of Romeo and Juliet* the two innocent lovers attempt to shun the spell of their cursed clan-name – all in vain.

It was their names and not their deed which dragged them to the abyss. For they cannot disentangle themselves from their viscous clan-names which connote descriptions of vendetta committed by the members of their clan – the guilt by association.

Juliet of Capulet laments that her lover Romeo of Montague is called "Montague".

> 'T is but thy name that is my enemy;
> Thou art thyself, though not a Montague.
> What's Montague? It is nor hand, nor foot,
> Nor arm, nor face, nor any other part
> Belonging to a man. O, be some other name!
> What's in a name? That which we call a rose
> By any other name would smell as sweet;
> So Romeo would, were he not Romeo call'd,
> Retain that dear perfection which he owes
> Without that title. Romeo, doff thy name,
> And for that name which is no part of thee,
> Take all myself.[1]

And Romeo of Montague wants to free himself, i.e., the denotation, from the name.

> By a name
> I know not how to tell thee who I am,
> My name, dear saint, is hateful to myself,
> Because it is an enemy to thee;
> Had I it written, I would tear the word.[2]

To be sure, "Capulet," "Montague" and "rose" in a sense, are all arbitrary designations. Since none of them are onomatopoetic signs, we can change the function given to these signs by the

---

[1] *The Tragedy of Romeo and Juliet*, Act II, Scene I, pp. 35–55.
[2] *Idem.*

community of speakers. However "Capulet" and "Montague" are even more arbitrary designations than the "rose." We would not violate any rule if we used any sign as a proper name. But if we call roses "stones," then we would violate our convention by calling them "roses."

Let us contrast here, similar words which Shakespeare put, in another play, in the mouth of Falstaff – this time by alluding that not all words are like proper-names (or what a proper name ought to be) a mere sound replaceable by others.

In *Henry IV*, the question is no more "What's in the name?" or "What's Montague?" but rather "What's in the word honour?" So says Falstaff:

Well, 'tis no matter, honour pricks me on.
Yea, but how if honour prick me off when
I come on? how then? Can honour
set to a leg? no: or an arm? no: or take
away the grief of a wound? no. Honour
hath no skill in surgery, then? no.
What is honour? a word. What is in that word
honour? What is that honour? air. A trim reckoning! Who
hath it? he that died a'Wednesday. Doth
he feel it? no. Doth he hear it? no. 'Tis
insensible, then? Yea, to the dead. But will
it not live with the living? no. Why?
detraction will not suffer it. Therefore I'll none
of it.[1]

The contrast is significant. "Montague" or "Capulet" are indeed names (though not a mere *flatus vocis*) and as such another name may replace each. Romeo does not participate in Montague-ness. Since a clan-name is not a property of a clan he may drop his clan-name. But "honour" is not a proper-name, and though the word "honour" is "an air" *honour* is not, and hence one may not dispose of it with impunity. Here we have a clear example of what is called by modern logicians "use-mention confusion."

I hinted darkly of the interest of the poets in what I called for the moment *connotation* and the *dual functions* of proper names.

[1] *Henry IV*, Part I, Act Fifth.

We shall see soon how the multifunctional aspects of proper names were regretted by some logicians and linguists and how theories were erected to correct this imaginary disaster. (Thus, the "logically proper-names" and the "sense-denotation aspects of names" of logicians, and "pure and impure names" of linguists).

Of magicians and their interests in proper-names (person-place names, numerals) it suffices to say that it stems from an ancient belief that proper-names are bounded by mysterious ties to things and persons which are their proper bearers[1] so that by envoking or abusing names one may cause beneficial or harmful changes in their bearers.

Let one entertain with Goethe the belief that:

A man's name is not like a cloak that merely hangs around him, that may be loosened and fightened at will. It's a perfectly fitting garment. It grows over him like his very skin. One cannot scrape and scratch at it without injuring the man himself,[2]

then one may as well go on believing that erasing a man's name would be tantamount to destroying the bearer of that name. Hence the injunction that "Thou shalt not take the Lord's name in vain" and warning that blasphemy, i.e., disrespectful mentioning of God's name, is a sin, that baptizing penguins is to make them Christian, and bestowing Saints' names on children is salutary, and what not. (That "Felicity" is conducive to felicity tells, if anything, something about Felicity's parents and nothing about her, even if she tries to live up to her name.)

I shall now leave the poets and magicians and concern myself with the works of the logicians and linguists in some detail.

The interest of the linguists and logicians in proper names often overlaps.

Concerned with the classification of words, a linguist wants to know whether there are significant differences between common-

---

[1] The belief that God is above name or that his names should not be used stems from the same superstition. Ferdowsi (the Persian poet) begins *The Epic of the Kings* in the name of God. Yet in the same poem he announces that God is above name:
"In the name of the Lord of Life and Wisdom
(Beyond this, thought bypasses not)
He who is above name, fancy and sign,
He who is the maker of the essence sublime.
With thy eyes, if thou cannot see God —
Pray: do not hurt thy two eyes."
[2] *Dichtung und Wahrheit.*

names or appelatives and proper-names. This will not only help grammarians but linguists as well who need to know in their study of the structure of a new language what kind of an expression are proper names. (Thus we have a theory that a proper name, in *any language*, must designate an object meeting a condition of spatiotemporal contiguity in such a way that there be a many-one-relation between the utterance of that expression and a particular entity.)

Concerned with the problems of inferring and referring a logician wants to know whether proper names are meaningful expressions or merely expressions without connoting attributes or whether they are substitutable by sentences called the definite descriptions, and if they are meaningful expressions whether we can infer something about the bearer of the name by hearing its name.

Despite their overlapping areas of interest logicians and linguists are often ignorant of each other's work. Many logicians such as Mill, Frege, and Russell, being unaware of the difficulties which a linguist faces in trying to classify various and heterogeneous expressions which go under the heading of proper-names, made blunders by talking about obvious cases and ignoring more complicated ones. They show very little awareness that not all proper names are as simple as Personal-First-Names or as fictitious names. Some logicians went so far as to construct theories about proper names without paying the least attention to some facts about names already well known to grammarians.

On the other hand many linguists and grammarians who have done hard work on the problem of the classification of nouns manifest ignorance of some important works done by logicians. They assume, for example, that a proper name is easily definable in terms of the description of its bearer – or they try offering definitions without being aware of the hazards of the definition, which are well known to logicians. Thus, we have philosophically naive statements of otherwise able linguists and grammarians, namely Sir Alan Gardiner or Otto Jesperson and, of late, H. S. Sørensen.

The interest of logicians in proper-names is connected with the following problems:

First: The metaphysical dichotomy of Universal-Particular has correspondent grammatico-semantical categories of Common-Name-Proper-Name. It is assumed that a Proper-Name is a name of a particular entity or substance and a Common-Name is the name of properties which are universal and are assigned to a substance.

Second: The general theories of meaning such as Denotation-Connotation, or Sense-Denotation, or the Use theory called forth attention to the function of words, including proper-names. Moreover, the contrast between Common-Names, which was correlated with Universals, and Proper-Names, which are supposed to denote Particulars, was regarded as helpful to understanding the function of common-names.

Third: It was believed by some philosophers not only that the meaning of a proper name is or ought to be the object which is denoted by it (and it was not always clear whether the belief is a prescription or a description) but also that words are essentially proper names and hence if one word is used on different occasions, there must be one identical object present which it denotes. Thus proper name is used as the model for explaining the meaning of quite dissimilar categories such as common-names, adjectives, and relations.

In this work my concern is neither with the semantic problem with regard to the meaning of common-nouns nor with the metaphysical theories concerning Universals and Particulars, (I dealt with these issues in *Universals: A New Look at an Old Problem*) but solely with semantico-grammatical theories of logicians and linguists concerning proper names.

We shall start first with logicians and will critically examine theories offered by Mill, Frege, and Russell, and comments made of late by Ziff, Ayer, Strawson, and others.

As a reminder note that a logician while doing pure logic is not concerned either with proper or common-names. He may face the problem, however, when he is confronted with the issue of substituting constants for variables and, in general, with questions concerning the application of his system.

In a deeper level, however, the very categories of *constant* and *variable* were borrowed from grammatical categories of proper name and common name.

As evidence in support of this contention I refer to Alonzo

Church's system of logic. Church writes that "In the formalized language which we study, the nearest analogues of the common name will be *variable* and *form* ... we wish to preserve the distinction of a proper name, or constant, from a form which is concurrent to a constant ... the term *constant* becomes synonymous with *proper name having a denotation*." In his system Church adopts a theory of names which is due "in its essential to Gottlob Frege," even though he readily admits that "There is not yet a theory of the meaning of proper names upon which general agreement has been reached as the best." [1]

---

[1] Church, A., *Introduction to Mathematical Logic*, Vol. I. Princeton, 1956 pp. 3–4, 9.

II. THEORIES OF LOGICIANS

1. Mill

Mill considers words to be *names* and "all names" according to him are "names of something, real or imaginary." [1] He regards expressions as different as "John," "virtue," "old age," "humanity," "God," "man" or even definite descriptions such as "The king who succeeded William the Conqueror," or "Caesar's army" (his own examples) all as Names.

Names are then divided by him into two classes of *Individual Name*, i.e., "a name which is only capable of being truly affirmed, in the same sense, of one thing" and *General Name*, i.e., "name which is capable of being truly affirmed, in the same sense, of each of an infinite number of things."

Names are again divided into two classes of *Connotative Name*, i.e., "one which denotes a subject (anything which possesses attributes), and implies an attribute" and *Non-Connotative Name*, i.e., "names which signify a subject only or an attribute only."

Once more names are divided into *Concrete Name*, i.e., "names which stand for a thing," and *Abstract Name*, i.e., "names which stand for an attribute of a thing."

Now proper-names (henceforth P-Ns) fall under the classes of Individual, Non-Connotative, and Concrete names.

---

[1] All references are to Mill's *A System of Logic*, 10th ed. (first published in 1843), Book 1, chaps. 1 and 2. Longmans, Greene Co., London, 1879.

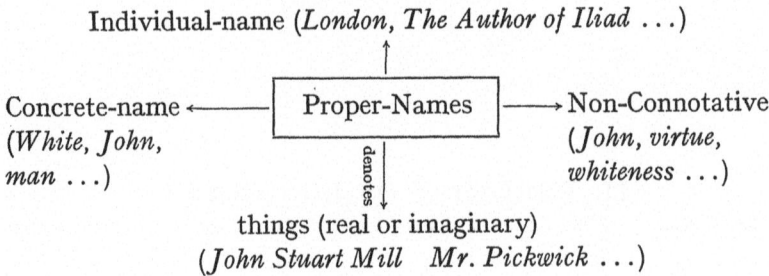

Individual-name (*London, The Author of Iliad . . .*)

Concrete-name ←——— | Proper-Names | ——→ Non-Connotative
(*White, John,*   (*John, virtue,*
man . . .)   *whiteness . . .*)

denotes

things (real or imaginary)
(*John Stuart Mill   Mr. Pickwick . . .*)

Explication of the Theory

First: To say that PNs are individual names is not to say that
the same name may not be given to different persons and places.
But only that they are not given to them (unlike the common
names) *qua* their common properties. "It is not conferred upon
them to indicate any qualities or anything which belongs to them
in common in any *sense* at all, consequently not in the same sense."

Second: To say that PNs are non-connotative is to say that
they do not indicate or imply (unlike common nouns) any attributes as belonging to these individuals. "When we name a child
by the name Paul or a dog by the name Caesar, these names are
simply marks used to enable those individuals to be made subject
of discours. It may be said, indeed that we must have some
reason for giving those names rather than any other – but the
name, once given is independent of the reason. A man may have
been named John, because that was the name of his father; a
town may have been named Dartmouth, because it is situated at
the mouth of the Dart. But it is no part of the signification of the
word John, that the father of the person so called has the same
name; nor even of Dartmouth, to be situated at the mouth of the
Dart – for otherwise, when the fact ceased to be true, no one
would any longer think of applying the name."

Third: PNs are not connotative signs; that is, they convey no
information about the bearers of those signs and hence are names
without signification or simply "unmeaning marks."

"Whenever the names given to objects convey any information,
that is, whenever they have properly any meaning, the meaning
resides not in what they *denote*, but in what they *connote*. The only

names of objects which connote nothing are *proper names*, and these have, strictly speaking, no signification."

Fourth: PNs are signs, i.e., purposeful configurations of sounds or letters. However, Mill insists that they are meaningless, i.e., non-connotative marks. "If, like the robber in the Arabian Nights, we make a mark with chalk on a house to enable us to know it again, *the mark has a purpose, but it has not properly any meaning* – when we impose a proper name, we perform an operation in some degree analogous to what the robber intended in chalking the house. A proper name is but an *unmeaning mark* which we connect in our minds with the idea of the objects, in order that whenever the mark meets our eyes we may think of that individual object. Not being attached to the thing itself, it does not, like the chalk enable us to distinguish the object when we see it, but it *enables us to distinguish* when it is spoken of. When we predicate of anything its proper name, when we say, pointing to a man, this is Brown or Smith, or pointing to a city, that it is York, we *do not merely by so doing convey to the reader any information about them, except that they are their names*." (Italics mine)

Fifth: Some expressions which are used as PNs are not genuine PNs but are disguised descriptions and that is why they are meaningful expressions. "'The Sun' or 'God' when used by a monotheist are indeed descriptions, since however they may be *in fact* predicable only of one object, *there is nothing in the meaning of the words themselves which implies this* ... we may speak of many suns ... and many gods."

On the other hand, there are definite descriptions which, because of their grammatical forms, guarantee the uniqueness of the referent such as "the only son of John Stiles," or "the author of the Iliad." In such cases "the employment of the article *the* implies" uniqueness of the referent, "though it is conceivable that more than one might have participated in the authorship of Iliad."

Mill's theory contains some germs of truth, which were neglected by his critics, and some blunders which were magnified.

First: His assertions that the use of a PN, like the use of the definitive description, presuppose that the speaker is referring to one and only one object, i.e., individual, is correct. After all, a PN differs from a common noun by its referring function which uniquely determines its referent.

Second: Mill asserts correctly that the use of a PN enables us to distinguish "the thing itself" (i.e., bearer of the name) when it is spoken of.

Third: Mill recognizes, though obliquely, that PNs are not mere noises or a mere configuration of letters, but are meaning-bearing sounds, i.e., signs. To convey to some one that a sound is a PN and not a mere noise, we may point to a person or a place and utter that sound. And Mill does not deny that uttering a sound and pointing to things may convey information, i.e., "that they are their names."

However, Mill never develops these interesting remarks; rather he returns to the moot point that PNs are unmeaning signs, e.g. "non-connotative."

One may wonder why, if a mark does have such an important function, should Mill insist that nevertheless it is a meaningless mark?

Mill makes three important mistakes. First is his basic view that words are essentially names and hence either they are denotative signs like PNs, or connotative like common nouns. This view is severely criticized by others.

The second mistake is to identify meaning with connotation. Mill having identified meaning with connotation, is forced to deny meaning to PNs. PNs, in contrast to some other individual names such as definite descriptions, or in contrast to common-nouns, "implies no attribute" and hence are taken to be unmeaning signs.

However, the meaning of a sign is not its connotation. "Connotation" is a psycho-linguistic concept having to do with the associations of a name with some extra-linguistic entities which the hearer sometimes makes upon hearing a name.

The third mistake is that Mill takes PNs to be mere signs which are designed to be used if the occasion arises and thus he takes them in their pure form. However, *used* proper names are not without informative power ("connotation" in Mill's language). That is, one may infer something about the bearer of the name by knowing how the name is actually used in a certain context. "John," for example, is an English first name of a male and "Oxford" is an English name of a place. Even if we do not know that "John" is a first name of a male we may infer from "John shaved his beard" that a person-male is talked about. Or from "I am going to Oxford" that Oxford is a name of a place if not a name of a university or a ford for oxen.

It is true as Mill insists that these connotations are "not part of the signification" of the name. Nonetheless, when a PN is systematically used it acquires some informative force which is due to its connection with its bearer. "John" is used in English usually as a name for a person-male, though we would not violate *any* rule if we bestow it on a dog or as Russell did on a chalk-mark.[1]

We agree with Mill that a PN is used as a name for an individual (though it could be used as a common noun) – that it is used as a sign for the identification and distinction of a particular entity. But contra Mill we argue that PNs are not mere noises but signs with a distinctive function like any other words in a language. Apart from the fact that PNs do have meaning, we shall argue that they could have informative power. The proper and systematic use of a PN could convey information about the bearer of the name; but this information should not be identified with meaning of the PN. The meaning of a PN is a constant feature of a certain sign, but the informative feature of that sign is variable. Since in English there is no systematic way of assigning a PN, i.e., one may call, as Mill observes, his dog "Ceasar." From a bare mentioning of a name we cannot infer information about its bearer. However, if a sign is used in a context we should be able to recognize its function, e.g., that it is a verb or a name.

2. Frege

In philosophical literature references are given to Frege's semantic theory which includes a discussion of PNs. It should be mentioned, however, that Frege was not concerned with explication of the function of PNs in natural language. For this reason objections which were brought forth against Frege's theory by some linguists (like those directed against Russell's theories which were designed primarily as solutions of some logical or epistomological puzzles) on the ground that the theory is not true to the facts of language or speech are otiose.

Nevertheless, since Frege's semantic theory in an oblique way

---

[1] See under "Russell."

illuminates some problems with regard to PNs, a brief discussion of his theory will follow.

Let us mention some of these problems.

First: Let us assume that PNs are meaningless words on the ground that:

a. A PN unlike a common-name does not have a connotation.
b. That in ordinary language it seems odd if we ask for the meaning or a meaning of x if x is replaced by a personal name or a place name (unless the PN was originally meant to be a description).
c. That PNs do not appear essentially in dictionaries, and we do not translate or paraphrase PNs as we do other words.
d. That ignorance of a man's name is not ignorance of the language and knowledge of his name is not knowledge of a language.

This assumption has an undesirable consequence, i.e., that a change of a name in a sentence should not change the meaning of that sentence. But obviously PNs are not meaningless noises since their use in a sentence, like the use of other words, does contribute to the meaning of the sentence in which they enter. If in a sentence a PN is replaced by another expression which is not synonymous with it, it changes the meaning of that sentence. In this respect PNs are just like other words. The problem is then what is the meaning of PNs (in distinction from the meaning of other words, notably common names)?

Second: Suppose that we identify meaning of a PN with the object which it denotes and argue that we do change the meaning of a sentence if we substitute another name for a name which occurs in that sentence since each name may denote a different denotation. Thus in a sentence, "Hitler committed suicide" if we substitute "Stalin" for "Hitler" we will have a different sentence since "Hitler" denotes the dictator of Germany (1934–1945) and "Stalin" the dictator of U.S.S.R. (1922–1953).

Third: However, if we identify the meaning of a PN with its denotation then as Wittgenstein says it would be nonsensical to say "'Mr. N. N. is dead.' For when Mr. N. N. dies one says that the bearer of the name dies, not that the meaning dies ... for if the name ceased to have meaning it would make no sense to say 'Mr. N. N. is dead'." [1]

---

[1] Wittgenstein, *Philosophical Investigations*, Basil Blackwell, par. 38.

It follows that the sentence "Hitler committed suicide" is meaningless if we identify meaning of "Hitler" with Hitler. Thus both assumptions, i.e., that PNs are meaningless or that the meaning of PNs are the things denoted by them lead to absurdity.

Now Frege's semantic theory which appears in his famous article *On Sense and Nominatum*,[1] though it deals primarily with the role of PNs in an artificial language, solves the problem which arises from identifying the meaning of a PN with its denotation.

Frege insists that for the sake of clarity and avoidance of incorrect inference, "It is to be demanded that in a logically perfect language (logical symbolism) every expression constructed as a proper name in a grammatically correct manner and of already introduced symbols in fact designate an object; and that no symbol be introduced as a proper name without assurance that it have a nominatum ... It deem it at least as appropriate to issue a warning against *apparent* proper name that have no nominatum."

Frege distinguishes between genuine PNs and the apparent PNs. A genuine PN is an expression having both nominatum or referent and sense, whereas an *apparent* PN has only a sense.

The sense of a PN is a contribution (Beitrag) made by that name to the thought expressed by the sentence of which it is a part. A genuine PN like "Aristotle" may have different senses such as "the teacher of Alexander the Great" or "the Stagirite disciple of Plato." However, "as long as the nominatum remains the same, these fluctuations in sense are tolerable. But they should be avoided in the system of a demonstrative science and should not appear in a perfect language."

A "sense" of a PN, unlike the associated images of the nominatum of that PN which are variable and subjective, is objective and determinable and hence ought to be distinguished from what is called the "connotation" of the name.

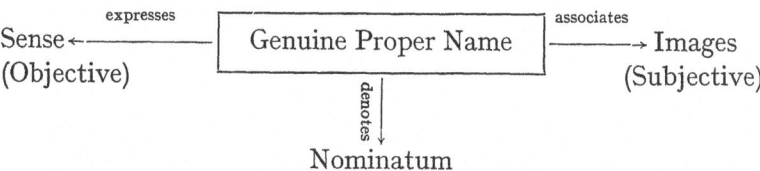

[1] Frege, all references are to "On Sense and Nominatum," *Reading in Philosophical Analysis*, eds. Feigl and Sellars, Appleton-Century, 1949.

That a genuine PN does designate is according to Frege a "presupposition" of any assertion in which a PN is used. Thus, if we take the statement "Odysseus deeply asleep was disembarked at Ithaca" to be either true or false, then "Odysseus" should denote someone.

However, Frege writes, "So long as we accept the Homeric poem as a work of art it does not matter whether 'Odysseus' has a nominatum." It is enough that it has sense.

So arguing Frege solved his own puzzle about identity, i.e., what makes some identity statements non-trivial. To say, for example, that "Cicero is Tully" is not to say trivially that "Cicero is Cicero," but to say that the two PNs "Cicero" and "Tully" both have one nominatum while having two senses. [Notice that the sentence "Cicero is Tully" only looks like an identity statement. The full name of the famous Roman orator is "Marcus" (praenomen) "Tullius" or "Tully" (nomen) "Cicero" (cognomen), i.e., nickname given by friends. Thus instead of a pseudo-identity statement of some logicians (not Frege, however), i.e., "Cicero is Tully," we should say "'Cicero' is a nickname of Tully," which is not an identity assertion.] [1]

Frege also solved the problem with regard to the significant use of referentless names. A PN whether pseudo or genuine expresses its sense and as such it may be significantly used without having a referent. However, we shall note the following difficulties in Frege's account of PN.

First: Frege assumes that a genuine PN is an embodied name and an apparent PN has a soul, i.e., a sense; whereas there is no guarantee that if a PN is genuine it should have a bearer and a sense, or that if it is not, it must have a sense. Of course, if we *use* an expression as a PN, namely in order to identify uniquely an entity, then it follows vacuously that someone or something is being identified and hence we may talk about the referent or the sense of that expression. But from the fact that an expression *purports* to be used as a referring expression it does not follow that it does in fact have a referent or sense. As a matter of fact, there

---

1 Thus Quine writes: "To rid language of redundant nomenclature of the simple type, e.g., 'Tully' and 'Cicero,' would be no radial departure; but to eliminate redundancies among complex names ... would be to strike at the roots." *Methods of Logic*, p. 209.

are proper PNs which are never used (for example, some of the first names listed in books which French citizens are legally obligated to use when naming the newborn) and there are also obsolete names, etc.

The contrast with Mill is instructive. Mill, as we observed, takes PNs as if they are all listed in books waiting to be tagged on things, hence his insistence upon the lack of meaning of PNs. Frege, on the other hand, looks at PNs as if they have already been used and thus his emphasis on their having a sense-denotation or at least a sense (in case of apparent PNs).

Second: Even if we assume that all PNs have been used it is still wrong to identify the meaning of a PN with its sense.

To talk about the "sense" of a PN is to talk about the various properties of its bearer in case the name is a personal name; or about the imaginary properties of an imaginary bearer in case the PN is a fictional name. Now it is true that "Scott" is the name among others of, "the author of Waverley," "Venus" is the name of the morning star and "Bucephalus" is a name of the war horse of Alexander the Great. However, all these expressions are used as names and could be used to refer to various objects.

In each case, the meaning of a name should be distinguished from the properties of its bearer.

Frege's theory is an attempt to explain why it is not always trivial to assert identity statements by linking a PN with another PN or with a unique property of its denotation. But it does not help us much to answer the question what is the meaning of a PN, except negatively, by showing that the denotation of a name is not its meaning.

3. Russell

Russell's interest in PNs has been always connected with his logical and epistemological theories. However, some linguists have taken Russell's statements to be intended as a description of the linguistic facts and criticized him without realizing that Russell's statements like Frege's are not intended to comprise a linguistic theory – though Russell is not always explicit about his undertaking.

Despite this, Russell's view deserves close attention and will help us in understanding of the nature of a PN.

I will try to present Russell's view on PN with a minimum attention to its logical and epistemological concomitant. Let us mention at least this much that Russell has been continually concerned with the problem of meaning and meaning has often been regarded by him to be a kind of referring.

Now since PNs and the definite descriptions are typical referring expressions, it is assumed that the proper use of these expressions guarantee the existence of referents which are the constituants of the world. The problem than was to explain the meaning of some PNs and some definite descriptions which do not have ostensible referents. The theory of definite description is thus devised to show that we may still talk meaningfully about such things as Unicorn, or the present king of France, without committing ourselves to a belief in existence or subsistence of such bogus entities.

In his article written for *Monist*, in 1918, Russell [1] defines PN as:

1. "Proper Name – word for particular. Definition" There follows immediately a warning that this definition "as far as common language goes, . . . is obviously false."

2. This definition is a preparation for a definition of atomic propositions, viz., propositions in which particulars are named.

3. Now to refer to a particular, but not to describe it, we need a PN. We may refer to a particular, like a dot on the blackboard, by "this." However if we call it "John," we can refer to it later.

4. Ordinary names like "Socrates" and "Plato," though, "originally intended to fulfill this function for standing for particular" are "really abbreviations for descriptions" since they are used in the absence of their bearers.

5. It follows that, "A name, in the narrow logical sense of a word whose meaning is a particular, can only be applied to a particular with which the speaker is acquainted. Because you cannot name anything you are not acquainted with. You remember, when Adam named the beasts, they came before

---

[1] Russell, "The Philosophy of Logical Atomism," also appeared in *Logic and Knowledge*, ed. R. C. Marsh, p. 323, London: Allen Unwin, 1951.

him one by one, and he became acquainted with them and named them."

This theory led Russell to a conclusion that "in strict logical sense," logically PNs are words like "this" or "that."

Like Mill's PNs, "this" and "that" indicate objects without attributing any property to them. So to speak, they are the name of bare particulars. In this way singular demonstrative pronouns, which like PNs are uniquely referring expressions, were assimilated to PNs, despite the fact that they differ from PNs.

Wittgenstein regards this assimilation as a kind of confusion: "If you do not want to produce confusion you will do best not to call these words names at all – yet, strange to say, the word "this" has been called the only genuine name, so that anything else we call a name was only in an inexact approximate sense.

This queer conception springs from a tendency to sublime the logic of our language – as one might put it. The proper andwer to it: we call very different things "names"; the word "name" is used to characterize many different kinds of use of a word, related to one another in many different ways; but the kind of use that "this" has is not among them." [1]

Sir Alan Gardiner, a linguist, similarly objects to Russell's statements about logically proper names. Not being aware of Russell's philosophy of logical atomism, Gardiner assumes that Russell is talking about PNs in natural language. He objects, "Philologists will be amazed to find *this* parading as a proper name, since one has only to place *John* and *this* alongside one another to realize that they are words of entirely different caliber." [2]

This objection has a force if Russell was concerned with description of how pronouns or PNs are actually used in language. Russell, however, makes it clear from the outset that he is not interested in such things.

While Gardiner and some other linguists were mistaken about the import of Russell's early proposals Alonzo Church gives a true appraisal of it. He writes "The doctrine of Russell amounts very nearly to a rejection of proper names as irregularities of the

[1] *Ibid.*, par. 40.
[2] Gardiner, A. H., *The Theory of Speech and Language*, Oxford: Clarendon, 1932, p. 60.

natural languages which are to be eliminated in constructing a
formalized language. It falls short of this by allowing a narrow
category of proper names which must be names of sense qualities
that are known by acquaintance, and which, in Fregean terms,
have *Bedeutung* and not *Sinn*," [1]

Russell Like Frege takes the ordinary PNs as those which are
actually used and hence he regards them to be descriptions. Thus
in the words of Urmson, "So words like 'this' were called logically
proper names as doing what ordinary proper names set out
unsuccessfully to do." [2]

The invention of logically PNs is connected with Russell's
epistemological theory. His logically PN is meant to be a kind of
referring expression which guarantees the existence of things we
are acquainted with. We should not assume, however, that
Russell commits the sin of ontologizing, i.e., that the use of
logically PNs necessitated the existence of objects. Rather, he
makes it clear that part of his definition of "true proper name" is
that it should refer to something. So he writes in another place:
"In the case of a true proper name, the name is meaningless unless
it names something, and if it names something, that something
must occur. This may seem reminiscent of the ontological
argument, but it is really only part of the definition of 'name.' A
proper name names something of which there are not a plurality
of instances, and names it by a convention *ad hoc*, not by a
description composed of words with previously assigned meanings.
Unless, therefore, the name names something, it is an empty
noise, not a word." [3]

We should also notice that though Russell at one time talked
about ordinary PNs as abbreviations for descriptions, he argued
later, that both in practice and theory PNs are indispensable.

He writes, "We cannot wholly dispense with proper names by
means of co-ordinates. We can perhaps reduce the number of
proper names, but we cannot avoid them altogether. Without
proper names we can express the whole of theoretical physics, but
no part of history and geography." [4]

---

[1] *Ibid.*, p. 4.
[2] Urmson, J. D., *Philosophical Analysis*, Oxford: Clarendon, 1951, p. 85.
[3] Russell, *An Inquiry into Meaning and Truth*, London: George Allen, 1940, p. 32.
[4] Russell, *Human Knowledge*, New York: Simon and Schuster, 1948, p. 78. For the

To show that descriptions are not substitutes for PNs he gives the following arguments:

"Somebody must be the tallest man now living in the U.S. Let us suppose he is Mr. A. We may then, in place of 'Mr. A.' substitute 'the tallest man now living in the U.S.,' and this substitution will not, as a rule alter the truth or falsehood of any sentence in which it is made. But it will alter the statement. One may know things about Mr. A. that one does not know about the tallest man in the U.S., and vice-versa. One may know that Mr. A. lives in Iowa, but not know that ... This illustrates, once more, that there are same things which cannot be expressed by means of descriptions substituted for names." [1]

This point is important, since only recently a linguist (H. S. Sørensen) has tried to define PNs in terms of the descriptions of their bearers, and some philosophers unduly criticized Russell for holding throughout the belief that PNs are simply abbreviations for descriptions. Thus Ayer in 1963 writes: "The fact that proper names do not have any fixed connotation makes it technically wrong to say, as Russell does, that they are abbreviations for descriptions, if what is understood here by is some piece of information which individuates the bearer of the name. The statement that Sir William Hamilton was a Scotsman cannot be equivalent to the statement that the man who invented the quantification of the Predicate was a Scotsman even when it is put forward by someone who knows nothing else about him. For it is a not necessary truth that Sir William Hamilton invented the Quantification of the Predicate." [2]

Gardiner also assumes that Russell identified PNs with descriptions. He objects:

"The word *Socrates* is a mere sound-label, and as such is an *alternative* to any description of Socrates complete enough to identify him, but is not a description itself ... All that the word *Socrates* tells us when it is pronounced is that reference is being made to a certain entity called *Socrates*. To apply the term 'description' to a word which may indeed awaken the memory of

most recent opinion of Russell on this subject, see chap. III of this book entitled, "Proper Names," p. 72–84.

[1] *Idem.*

[2] Ayer, A. J., "Names and Descriptions" in *The Concept of a Person*, St. Martin's Press, 1963, p. 142.

sundry bits of information but which does not itself point to any one of them is a strange abuse of terms." [1]

Another linguist, i.e., N. Chomsky, criticizes Russell's proposal about PNs as if it is made with the intention to describe a linguistic fact.

Russell wrote in *An Inquiry:*

> From a logical point of view, a proper name may be assigned to any continuous portion of space-time (Macroscopic continuity suffices). Two parts of one man's life may have different names; for instance, Abram and Abraham, or Octavianus and Augustinus. "The Universe" may be regarded as a proper name for the whole of space-time ... It may therefore be assumed, at least for the present, that every proper name is the name of a structure, not of something destitute of parts. But this is an empirical fact, not a logical necessity. [2]

Chomskey objects to Russell (after quoting a part of the paragraph) that:

> There is no logical necessity for names or other ' object words" to meet any condition of spatiotemporal contiguity or to have other Gestalt qualities, and it is a nontrivial fact that they apparently do insofar as the designated objects are of the type that can actually be perceived (for example, it is not true of ' United States").
>
> There is no a priori reason why a natural language could not contain a word "HERD," like the collective "herd" except that it denotes a single scattered object with cows as parts, so that ' a cow lost a leg" implies "the herd lost a leg," etc. [3]

Such objections to Russell's theory are captious. Russell's view on PNs may be summarized as the following:

1. Ordinary PNs, before being assigned to particulars, are just signs without connotation. We may bestow a name upon any particular.

2. However, as soon as a thing is named it acquires as part of the meaning of its name some properties of its bearer, i.e., will degenerate into description. This is because its bearer is something possessing some properties. It is possible to produce many true descriptions of the same bearer of a name.

[1] *Ibid.*, p. 64.
[2] Russell, *Inquiry*, pp. 33–34.
[3] Chomsky, N., *Aspects of the Theory of Syntax*, The M.I.T. Press, 1965, p. 201.

3. Definite descriptions may be used in lieu of a PN. But they are not logically equivalent.
4. Logically PNs are names of bare particulars which we are directly acquainted with. They alone indicate an object without ascribing characteristics to it.

Thus Russell disagrees with Mill that an ordinary PN is without a connotation. We may sometimes use various descriptions of a bearer of a PN in lieu of it. However, his invented logically PN coincides with Mill's idea of PN.

4. Some More Recent Talk on Proper Names

I now leave behind the theories of Mill, Frege and Russell and will concentrate upon some more recent views offered by philosophers who are interested in the problems of meaning and referring. We shall see that though these views are unsystematic and are often stated as subsiduary to other issues they contain some fresh insights and hence require close attention.

I shall first state and evaluate the more systematic accounts of PN given by Ziff and Strawson, and then some other views of various writers such as Ayer, Searle, Kneale, Shawayder and others.

(i) Ziff

In his book *Semantic Analysis* Ziff offers some opinions on PNs. His remarks, however, are both illuminating and puzzling. He begins with a necessary warning that, "it is not possible to state a simple strong generalization about proper names. One can only say what is so for the most part and that must be qualified." [1]

Two problems seem to interest Ziff.

First: Whether there are semantic regularities, i.e., "regularities of some sort to be found in connection with the corpus pertaining to both linguistic elements and then to other things, e.g., the utterances and situations, or to phrases and persons, as well as to utterances and utterance," [2] in connection with PNs and if so, what kind.

---

[1] Ziff, P., all references are to *Semantic Analysis*, Cornell University Press, New York, 1960, p. 93.
[2] *Ibid.*, p. 27.

Second: Suppose there is no regularity to be found in connection with PNs – should we agree with Frege and others that they are meaningful expressions, or consent to Mill's view that they are meaningless?

With regard to the first question Ziff argues first that there is a sort of regularity, "generally speaking, a fairly reliable indication of the occurrence of a proper name as an utterance is that there be a many-one-relation between the utterance and a particular spatiotemporal entity ..." [1]

This suggestion, however, is rejected on the ground that it does not provide a necessary condition for an expression to be counted as a PN. "'I shall do a picture of Pegasus' cannot be related to a particular spatiotemporal entity yet the proper name 'Pegasus' occurs in that utterance. And 'Smith' is a proper name yet it cannot be related to one and only one particular spatiotemporal entity." [2]

With regard to the second problem, he seems first to be rejecting the view held by many, that PNs are meaningful expressions. For he writes:

The fact that "Witchgren" (the names of his imaginary cat) in "Witchgren is on the mat" does contrast with "he," "dust," ' water," is I believe the principal reason why so many philosophers are inclined to suppose that proper names do have meaning in English. And if one adopts the slogan, that "the meaning of a word is its use in the language," one can hardly avoid supposing that proper names generally do have meaning in English. [3]

To the question "What's in a name?" he answers,

There is nothing in a proper name. It has an information content but even so, it is all sound and if the sound is changed the name is changed. [4]

The conclusion seems to be, "For the most part then, proper names are not said to have meaning in English or to have a meaning in English. But certain proper names are said to mean something to someone and certain proper names are said to have meaning." [5]

[1] *Ibid.*, p. 89.
[2] *Idem.*
[3] *Ibid.*, p. 173.
[4] *Ibid.*, p. 175.
[5] *Ibid.*, pp. 93–94.

Nevertheless, Ziff admits that PNs have a connotation though not meaning, i.e., some informative force.

> Even though I want to deny that proper names are, for the most part, said to have meaning in English ... I want to say that proper names do for the most part if not invariably have a connotation ... one can say that a proper name connotes something primarily to the hearer ...[1]

Ziff argues that,

> The difference between a proper name like "Witchgren" and a ' name,' or better a common noun, like ' tiger' in virtue of which only the latter can be said to have meaning in English (where meaning is of course merely a matter of connotation) is that: if there are two animals in a cage and one is a tiger, a perfect specimen of a tiger, and the other animal is virtually indistinguishable from it, then the second animal is a tiger. But if there are two animals in a cage and one is Witchgren and the other is virtually indistinguishable from it, it does not follow that the second animal is Witchgren. The two animals have been individuated in virtue of Witchgren's baptismal rites. (And that is the difference between ' names' like "rose" and ' Rose').[2]

That since there is a semantic regularity pertaining to the use of the expression "tiger" in English, we are able to determine whether an animal is a tiger or not. But since there is none with regard to the use of a PN we are not able to infer what the name of an animal is by looking at it.

Ziff, however, maintains earlier that there is some semantic regularity pertaining to the use of a PN.

> It's neither meaningless nor senseless to call a female cat "Charile" yet such a use of the name constitutes a deviation from a semantic regularity.[3]

(To which we may respond quoting Mill that "we name a dog by the name Ceaser").

I do not want here to question Ziff's account of semantic regularity which is an important part of his book. However, the following points have to be made.

First: The distinction between the meaning of an expression and the connotation which an expression may carry with itself

---

[1] *Idem.*
[2] *Ibid.,* p. 102.
[3] *Ibid.,* p. 33.

(which may awaken the memory of bits of information in the hearer's mind) – is significant. Whether PNs have meaning or not, it is important, as Ziff mentions, not to confuse meaning and connotation. (The same point is made by Frege.)

Second: Ziff takes PNs as if they all have been used, and not that they are kinds of expressions which *purport* to be used in a certain fashion. That is why he has trouble in establishing a semantic regularity with respect to the use of PNs. He is right. "'Smith' is a proper name yet it cannot be related to one and only one particular spatiotemporal entity." But why should we even try to make such a connection? It is enough to say that "Smith" is generally used as a personal name in English – that like all used personal names, it is given by some one as a kind of referring expression which uniquely individuates a person and that person usually caries his name through life and answers to it.

Here we may say that we have established a sort of regularity (not a semantic regularity) between a linguistic element, i.e., PNs, and its purported role, rather than between PNs and persons or places.

Indeed the pattern is very similar. Ziff writes, "if 'Hello' is uttered then generally one person is greeting one or more others." Likewise, we may say, "If 'Smith' is used then generally one person is uniquely referred to."

We do not have to relate a PN such as "Smith" or "Pegasus" or "Socrates," as Ziff tries unsuccessfully to do, to spatiotemporal entities. Rather, we should look at the function of PNs, i.e., the purpose which is assigned to PNs in language and appropriate conditions or regularities peculiar to their use. Such regularities, as we shall argue, are pragmatic rather than semantic.

Third: Ziff is wrong to insist upon the meaninglessness feature of PNs and in this he is open to the same objections which are brought against Mill.

We must agree with him that there is a vast difference between "rose" and "Rose." But not because the first is a meaningful expression since there is a semantic regularity pertaining to it, while the second is a meaningless expression since it is used arbitrarily as a PN and any other name will do as well. Now Ziff does not bluntly assert that PNs are meaningless. Rather, he talks obliquely – "I want to deny that proper names are, for the most part, said to have meaning in English ... For the time being, for this reason: not merely that we do not say so though that is relevant ..." [1]

However, it clearly follows from his theory in which meaning is identified with non-syntactic semantic regularities that PNs are meaningless expressions. If some types of utterances such as an ordinary surname like "Smith," fictional names like "Pegasus," or names of dead persons such as "Plato," or bygone places such as "Babylonia" do not have significant concommitant conditions, then upon his theory, they should be counted as meaningless expressions. From this alone it follows that there is something wrong with Ziff's theory of semantic-regularity. [2]

(ii) Strawson

Strawson has not been primarily concerned with the issue of PNs but mostly with definite descriptions. However, since the latter issue is closely connected with other referring expressions such as PNs, some discussion of PNs appear in his work.

To begin with, in *Introduction to Logical Theory*, Strawson rejects the view that the meaning of a genuine referring expression (such as definite descriptions which uniquely characterize some actual entities) is identical with the object to which it applies.

He also denies that there are any referring expressions whose use guarantees the existence of any object. Now PNs are typical referring-expressions. They are also incapable of satisfying the demand that their use require referents.

For where are genuine individual referring expressions to be found, having the characteristics required ... ? It might be though that proper names would fill the bill. But even a proper name does not satisfy the requirement that in order for a sentence in which it occurs to be significant there must exist just one individual which (or who) is its meaning. One can significantly ask, using a proper name, "Did N exist?" The same name can be borne by many different creatures or things; and in no case is the meaning of a name identical with a creature or thing which bears it. To bestow a name is not to give a word a meaning. [3]

---

[1] *Ibid.*, p. 94.

[2] For a rigorous criticism of this theory see "Review of Semantic Analysis," by J. J. Katz, Journal *Language*, volume 38, no. 1, pp. 52–69 (1962).

[3] Strawson, P., *Introduction to Logical Theory*, London: Methuen, 1952, p. 189.

Strawson concludes that no referring expression by itself, "even the so-called 'logically proper-name'," has a power to guarantee a referent.

Strawson argues in line with Wittgenstein that the so-called denotation theory of meaning does not explain even the meaning of a PN, not to speak of other expressions.

The meaning of a proper name is not to be identified with its purported denotation or with some uniquely determinable properties of its bearer.

This observation is cardinal, since not only some philosophers, but also some linguists, are committed to this theory.

In his famous article "On Referring" [1] Strawson classified PNs among expressions having a "uniquely referring use." Other groups of expressions belonging to this class are: singular demonstrative pronouns ("this" and "that"), singular personal and impersonal pronouns ("he," "she," "I," "you," "it") and phrases beginning with the definite article followed by a noun, qualified or unqualified, in the singular (e.g., "the table," "the old man," "the king of France").

Strawson recognizes that expressions belonging to these four groups may have other uses than a uniquely referring use.

Strawson in this article is primarily interested in the use of expressions belonging to the last class, namely the definite descriptions. However, what he says about the use of the definite descriptions could also have bearing upon the use of PNs.

Concerning the definite description like "The king of France," he writes:

When a man uses such an expression, he does not *assert*, nor does what he says *entail*, a uniquely existential proposition. But one of the conventional functions of the definite article is to act as a *signal* that a unique reference is being made ... When we begin a sentence with "the such-and-such" the use of "the" shows, but does not state, that we are intended to be, referring to one particular individual of the species "such-and-such." [2]

The same may be said of PNs. Thus, we may say, when a man uses a PN, he does not *assert*, nor does what he says *entail* that

[1] Strawson, P., "On Referring," *Philosophy and Ordinary Language*, ed. C. G. Caton, University of Illinois Press, 1963.
[2] *Idem.*

there is a unique entity, e.g., a person or a place, etc. But one of
the conventional functions of a PN is to act as a *signal* that a
unique reference is being made.

The function of a PN, in general, is to refer uniquely to an
entity; it does not guarantee that the PN has a bearer or if the
PN has a bearer does not indicate the ontological status of its
bearer. Numerous persons may carry the name "Smith." "Smith"
is not necessarily a name for a unique entity. But when we use
"Smith" we are, in general, referring uniquely to an entity. In
this respect "Smith" or "this" or "I" or "the king of France" are
all similar.

However, PNs differ from the other three referring expressions.
Strawson writes:

At one end of this scale stand the PNs we most commonly use in ordinary
discourse. The pure name has no descriptive meaning (except such as it
may acquire as a result of some one of its uses as a name). A word like "he"
has minimal descriptive meaning but has some. Substantial phrases like
"the round table" have the maximum descriptive force. An interesting
intermediate position is occupied by "impure" proper names like "The
Round Table" – substantial phrases which have grown capital letters.
Ignorance of a man's name is not ignorance of the language. That is why
we do not speak of the meaning of proper names. (But it won't do to say
they are meaningless.)

An ordinary personal name is, roughly, a word, used referringly, of
which the use is not dictated by any descriptive meaning the word may
have, and is *not* prescribed by any such general rule for use as a referring
expression (or a part of a referring expression) as we find in the case of
such words as "I," "this" and "the" but is governed by *ad hoc* conventions
for each particular set of applications of the word to a given person.

The important part is that the correctness of such applications does not
follow from any general rule or convention for the use of the word as such.[1]

[1] *Idem.* Here, in effect, Strawson comes close to secure meaning for PN, by observing "its referring use." However, in his earlier work, he criticizes Wittgenstein's
oblique statement that in the case of a PN, too, the meaning is the use. "Wittgenstein
attacks the notion of the word of which the meaning is the object it applies to: he
instances the ordinary proper name and distinguishes between its bearer and its
meaning (40); in this case, too, the *meaning* is the use (41–43). (Wittgenstein here
gives the wrong reason for objecting to the identification of the, or a, meaning of a
proper name with its bearer, or one of its bearers. If we speak at all of the meaning of
proper names, it is only in quite *specialized* ways, as when we say that 'Peter' means a
stone, or 'Giovanni' means 'John.' This is not an accident of usage, but reflects a
radical difference between proper names and other names. But here, as elsewhere,
Wittgenstein neglects the use of 'meaning')." "Review of Wittgenstein's Philosophical
Investigati ons," *Mind*, vol. LXIII, 1954.

I have quoted in some length to bring about the import of Strawson's remarks. That is:

First: PNs are among uniquely referring expressions.

Second: They are not meaningless, though we do not speak in English of the meaning of "Smith."

Third: Whereas the use of each pronoun or each definite description is determined by some linguistic rules, the use of PNs is governed by *ad hoc* conventions for each use. Thus, "John" is used in English as a personal first name of a male. However, no rule is violated if we use it as a surname, or a place-name or even a common noun (witness "John" used by Russell as a name of a chalk mark and "Quisling" as a name of *any* traitor during the Second World War).

These three points are important for a proper understanding of PNs. However, Strawson is not very clear when he writes about the lack of "descriptive meaning of pure PNs."

If PNs do have a referring-use then their meaning is established, and to speak of the lack of descriptive *meaning* of pure PNs is not helpful. Unless we include the properties of the bearer of a name as a part of the meaning of a name, it makes no sense to talk about pure PNs and of the lack of their descriptive meaning.

Strawson rightly observes that ignorance of a man's name is not ignorance of the language. This remark should be supplemented with another, i.e., "that ignorance that some expressions are used as PNs is ignorance of the language." We may not know someones name, but if we know English we should know that certain expressions which appear in a certain context are used as PNs and not as a preposition or verb, etc.

(iii) Ayer

In his recent article *Names and Description* Ayer raises the question: "What then is their (proper-names) meaning?" and answers, "This sounds a silly question – how could one answer it except by saying that as a rule different names have different meaning? If you will tell me what proper names you have in mind, then I will try to tell you what they severally mean." [1]

Next, he rejects the suggestion that the meaning of a PN is the

---

[1] *Idem.*

object which it denotes – and also a weaker assumption that "A proper name may not be thought to mean what it denotes, but is still held that it must denote something in order to be meaningful." For he argues that "the distinctive feature of the fictitious use of name ('Mr. Pickwick') is not that they have no reference, for this may also be true of names which are used historically, but that in what may be called their normal form the sentences in which they occur are not truth-claiming." [1]

Ayer comments on Strawson's statement that "a name is worthless without a backing of descriptions which can be produced on demand to explain its application" by saying that "to understand the use of a proper name one must know which individual it is intended to refer to, but this knowledge need not consist in the ability to furnish a verbal description of the individual in question. It may be enough that one picks out the right person or object, when the occasion arises." [2]

I believe that none of these statements enlarge our understanding of PNs.

We do not have to know anything about the individual Smith to be able to pick out the right person in order to know that "Smith" is used as a personal name. A name is not worthless without the backing of a description. But rather, as Wittgenstein observes, "Naming is a preparation for description. Naming is so far not a move in the language game any more than putting a piece in its place on the board is a move in chess." [3]

We do not bestow names on persons and places, artifacts, etc., if we are not interested to talk about them, i.e., to describe them or evaluate them, in general, to say something about the bearer of the name. Nonetheless, we should not assimilate the act of referring to a thing by using its name with the act of describing some facts about its bearer.

"Pickwick" is a fictitious name given by Dickens to one of his characters, and we may make many true as well as false statements about its bearer. Its bearer is not a historical figure, but a fictional one. We make mistakes only if we assume that our statements are descriptive of an historical figure. In each case, to

[1] *Idem.*
[2] *Idem.*
[3] *Ibid.*, par. 49.

talk about the bearer of a name, whether the name is fictional or
historical, is not the same thing as to talk about the use of the
bearer's name. Some writers do not talk about the *referent* of a
PN unless it is spatiotemporal. Russell, for example, writes:

> To say that unicorns have an existence in heraldry, or in literature, or in
> imagination, is a most pitiful and paltry evasion ... Similarly to maintain
> that Hamlet, for example, exists in his own world, namely, in the world of
> Shakespeare's imagination, just as truly as (say) Napoleon existed in the
> ordinary world, is to say something deliberately confusing ... There is
> only one world; the "real world." [1]

Still later (in *Human Knowledge*, p. 78) he writes:

> Let us take a person with whom we are not acquainted, say Socrates. We
> may define him as "the philosopher who drank the hemlock," but such a
> definition does not assure us that Socrates existed, and if he did not exist,
> "Socrates" is not a name.

Likewise, Quine writes, "The effort to preserve meaning for
'Cerberus' by presenting some shadowy entity for 'Cerberus' to
name is misdirected." (*Methods of Logic*, p. 199) However, there
is nothing wrong (unless we confuse various ontological levels and
hence Hamlet with Napoleon) in talking about referents of
"Hamlet" or "Zorotaster" or "Mr. Pickwick," or a numeral.
Referents need not be spatiotemporal – they may be a character
in a play, pseudo-historical person, a concept, a number, etc.

(iv) Searle

In his article on "Proper Names," [2] Searle makes the following
points.

1. PNs do not function as descriptions, but as pegs on which
   to hang descriptions. Though descriptions could be used,
   like PNs, to refer to an individual, they cannot perform the
   same functions. Since every time we use a description in
   place of a PN we have to specify identity conditions, i.e.,
   that two or more descriptions refer to the same thing.
2. Following Strawson he writes that "We may say that
   referring uses of both proper names and definite descriptions

---

[1] *Introduction to Mathematical Philosophy*, 2nd ed., London, 1926.
[2] Searle, J., "Proper Names," *Mind*, LXVII, no. 261, April, 1958.

presuppose the existence of one and only one object referred to."

3. Finally to the question: "Does a proper name have a sense?", he answers, "if this asks whether or not proper names are used to describe or specify characteristics of objects, the answer is 'No.' But if it asks whether or not proper names are logically connected with characteristics of the object to which they refer, the answer is 'Yes' in a loose sort of way."

Searle's familiar criticism of the substitutability of PNs with a definite description is correct. There may be many definite descriptions of the same person, and two people may give different descriptions of the same person. We need PNs if for no other reason than to convey the identity of someone to whom more than one definite description has been attributed. Thus as Searle writes PNs are like pegs on which we hang descriptions. The same point is made by Strawson. "It is proper names which tend to be the resting-places of reference to particulars, the points on which the descriptive phrases pivot." [1]

Searle's statements, however, with regard to the presupposition of the referring use of PNs are misleading.

The referring use of PNs does *not* "presuppose the existence of one and only one object referred to," but rather it *purports* to individuate one object referred to. Whether the object referred to exists spatiotemporally or in various ontological levels is not a presupposition of the referring use of PNs.

Searle's last mentioned point concerning the logical connection of a PN with properties of its bearer "in a loose sort of way" is weak. It is a contingent fact that names are usually not given without name-givers having an interest in the bearers of the names. But there is no logical connection, even in a loose sort of way, between a name and the bearer of that name.[2]

---

[1] Strawson, P., *Individual*, London, 1959, p. 58. (Methuen).

[2] More recently Searle writes: "anyone who uses a proper name must be prepared to answer the question 'who or what are you talking about?' and answers to this question, where adequate, will take the forms either of verbal identifying descriptions or of ostensive representations of the object." "Proper Names and Descriptions" p. 490 in *The Encyclopedia of Philosophy*, Vol. 6. 1967.

This still won't do. For suppose I ask you "Who is Churchill?" I am asking you to tell me something about the bearer of the name. If I knew the answer I would not have asked you. I may also use a name vacuously e.g., "Churchill is mortal or Chur-

(v) Shawayder

I would like now to consider some points which were made by Shawayder concerning PNs in his *Modes of Referring and The Problem of Universals*, and also in a review of a book of a Danish linguist, Sørensen, titled *The Meaning of Proper Names*.

1. He argues negatively, on familiar grounds, against the assimilation of a PN to description. Against Russell he writes,

But he should have concluded that a proper name, even in our usual sense of the term, quite apart from what its use presumes, is not itself a definite description at all.[1]

2. He argues that PNs do have meaning, since (a) "PNs, like other words, have their places in dictionaries" and (b) "They may be translated, even though sometimes are not. It is, for instance, interesting that PNs are seldom translated in literary works. Why? Well, 'Ivan' is a Russian name, it is to be expected that most people so-called are Russian, that the denotation of 'Ivan' is Russian is normally part of the meaning of 'Ivan'."[2]

I do agree with the contention that PNs do have meaning but not for his reasons, viz., that (a) they appear in dictionaries or that (b) they are translatable.

The ordinary dictionaries (even *The Oxford Dictionary of English Christian Names*) list some PNs and provide in place of definitions usually two items: (1) The etymology of the name. Since most English PNs (like PNs in other languages) were originally words in English, the dictionary indicates the meaning of such words. (Thus we see under Bernard (m): *Oger Berinhard*, compound of *berin* "a bear," *hard* "stern," following, the history

---

chill is not mortal," or ambiguously (as some logicians say) e.g., "John Doe" without being prepared to answer the question "who or what are you talking about?"

In using a PN what is necessary is to know that a sign is used as a name i.e., to make a unique reference to the same entity. It is not necessary to know anything about that entity. Note, for example how "John Smith" and "Mary Brown" are used in this passage, "The idea of Edward's being a clergyman, and living in a small parsonage house, diverted him beyond measure; and when to that was added the fanciful imagery of Edward reading prayers in a white surplice, and publishing the banns of marriage between John Smith and Mary Brown, he could conceive nothing more rediculous." Jane Austen *Sense and Sensibility*.

[1] Shawayder, D., *Modes of Referring and the Problem of Universals*, University of California Press, p. 59.

[2] Shawayder, D., "Review of the Meaning of Proper Names by H. S. Sørensen," *The Journal of Philosophy*, LXI – No. 15, August 6, 1964.

of the name, i.e., when it is introduced in English, changes in spelling, etc.) [1]

(2) Some description of some of the bearers of the name, if they are famous enough. (Thus under Cyrus (m) Gr ... from Persian Kuru, "throne," the name of the great king of Persia ...) [2]

None of these items constitute the meaning of a PN, since neither the etymology of a PN (or etymology of a word) is a part of the meaning of that word, nor is the description of some of its bearers (if a PN has any bearer). Here is a place where one may say that the *etymological* meaning of a word is *not* its use in language. This would not be in conflict with Wittgenstein's assertion that:

For a *large* class of cases – though not for all – in which we employ the word "meaning" it can be defined thus: the meaning of a word is its use in the language. [3]

Concerning the translation of PNs I disagree that we translate or need to translate PNs as such. We do, of course, translate some descriptions which are used as a name. Since these descriptions may contain information about their bearers, failure to translate deprives the reader of some information.

Thus titles such as *Great Expectations, Paradise Lost,* or a place name such as "The United States" or a nickname as "Shorty" are translated. However, PNs which are not descriptions, or if they were once descriptions they are no more, like "John," "Smith," or "Ivan," are not translatable, though they may be transliterated, i.e., represented or spelled in the characters of another alphabet.

Hence, it follows that what secures meaning for PNs are neither their occasional appearances in dictionaries nor the alleged fact about their translation.

(vi) Kneale

Finally, I would like to report some observations made by Kneale in his book *The Development of Logic.*

---

[1] Withycombe, E. G., *The Oxford Dictionary of English Christian Names,* London: Oxford Press, 1947, p. 25.

[2] *Ibid.,* p. 38.

[3] *Ibid.,* par. 43.

The following points about PNs are of interest:

1. "An ordinary proper name works like a definite description
   which has for its implication or presupposition the existence
   of something called by that name in the circle of the speaker
   and the hearer ... Proper names, like description, may
   admittedly be used sometimes without an implication of
   existence, i.e., when they are forced to commit suicide. But
   the fact that it seems slightly paradoxical to say 'Homer
   never existed' shows clearly that the normal use of a proper
   name presupposes the existence of something called by the
   name. Ordinary proper names and definite description ...
   their use implies, but does not guarantee, the existence of
   things of which they are designations." [1]

2. "There seems to be no imaginable context (other than of
   compiling a dictionary of names) in which the purposes
   served by the utterance of (PN) could not be served equally
   well by utterance of some paraphrase without a proper
   name." [2]

With regard to the first point we might repeat again that there
is no "implication" between the proper use of a proper name and
existence of its bearer. There is nothing paradoxical about saying
"Agamemnon never existed" or "There was no man called 'Robin
Hood'."

To argue that "ordinary proper names ... implies but does not
guarantee, the existence of things of which they are designations"
is to confuse the meaning of a referring expression with its
purported referent.

Concerning the second point I argue that there *are* not only
imaginable contexts but actual contexts in which the purpose
served by the utterance of a PN could *not* be served by utterance
of some paraphrase without a PN.

Suppose someone wants to convey the historical fact that
"Lenin" is an assumed cognomen for the leader of the October
Revolution – that Lenin's surname was "Ulianov" or someone
believes that the reason why Lenin abandoned his surname was

---

[1] Kneale, William and Martha, *The Development of Logic*, Oxford: The Clarendon
Press, 1962, pp. 597–598.
[2] *Ibid.*, p. 597.

that he could not pronounce his name. In each case, it is not possible to dispense with the name by using the description.

Consider again that someone wants to deny that "Shakespeare's real name was 'Bacon'." He could not express his view by saying merely that, "It is not the case that the real name of the author of Hamlet was the name of the author of The Novum Organum." Lastly consider the simple advertisement under *lost dogs* "answers to the name 'Dash': had on a brass collar." Here again the name is at least as important as any description of its bearer and perhaps more so, in case "Dash" is the name of a dog closely resembling many others.

The identification of the definite description with names generates paradoxes.

Kneale himself quoted a paradox which I believe was generated as a result of the assumption that the definite description of a certain number is identical with the name of that number.

The paradox which is called Berry's paradox, is, to quote Kneale:

concerns *the least integer not nameable in fewer than nineteen syllables.* Although it seems obvious that any name of this integer must contain at least nineteen syllables, the words printed above in italics amount to a name for it and they contain only eighteen syllables.[1]

At this point I would like to leave the theories and the pronouncements of logicians on PNs behind and provide at least a few samples of what some recent grammarians and linguists have written on this subject.

[1] *Ibid.*, p. 656.

III. THEORIES OF LINGUISTS

In this part I shall consider as a sample first theories offered by two linguists, namely, Sir Alan H. Gardiner and H. S. Sørensen and second, I shall mention some syntactic factors which were pointed out by a grammarian, viz., Otto Jesperson and others.

1. Gardiner

Gardiner, in his famous book *The Theory of Speech and Language*,[1] makes some remarks about PNs. Later, in *The Theory of Proper Names: A Controversial Essay*, he offers a theory. In both works, however, his view presupposes the correctness of the Saussure's Langue-Parole or Language – Speech dichotomy.

Gardiner defines "speech" as "a universally exerted activity, having at first definitely utilitarian aims. In describing this activity, we shall discover that it consists in the application of a universally possessed science, namely the science which we call language."

There are four elements in speech:

1. The speaker
2. The listener
3. The things referred to
4. The linguistic material

Now the speaker learns in a certain stage how to use the linguistic material (words) in order to achieve certain ends, e.g., to inform the listener that something is the case.

This theory is accepted by some philosophers. Thus Ryle,[2] in his

---

[1] *The Theory of Speech and Language.*
[2] Ryle, "Use, Usage and Meaning," *The Aristotelian Society*, Supplementary volume XXXV, 1961.

article *Use, Usage and Meaning*,[2] accepts this distinction and makes use of it in refuting a semantic view.

Ryle, using some economic analogy, tries to make the distinction clear. *Language*, Ryle says, is analogous to "a stock, fund or deposit of words, constructions, intonations, cliché phrases, and so on (is a corpus of teachable things ...) Whereas *Speech* or *discourse* is the activity or rather the clan of activities of saying things ... Roughly as Capital stands to Trade, so Language stands to Speech."

Now Ryle, like Gardiner, takes "words" to be units of language. They are like gold in banks having permanent purchasing power while in banks. But "sentences" are units of Speech. (from this Ryle deduces that while we may talk about use-misuse (solecistic) of words in a sentence, we should not talk about use-misuse of that sentence).

The Wittgensteinian injunction, "Don't ask for the meaning; ask for the use," according to Ryle "was a piece of advice to philosophers, and not to lexiographers or translators. It advised philosophers, ... when wrestling with some *a poria*, to switch their attention ... from their permanent purchasing-power while in the bank to the concrete marketing done yesterday morning with them to ... – from these words *qua* units of Language to live sentences in which they are being actively employed." [1]

Now since PNs are words in Language we should note how they have been employed in Speech. And to do this we may discover their function, just as we may discover the functions of other words.

Gardiner argues that PNs are words and not noises. He writes, "A proper name is a word, and being a word partakes of the fundamental two-sidedness of words as possessing both sound and meaning." [2]

To the question what is the meaning of PNs, he answers using an economic analogy.

If meaning be taken to signify simply "exchange-value," then obviously all PNs have meaning, since they are words and every word is a sound-sign standing for something, this something being its exchange-value.[3]

---

[1] *Idem.*
[2] *Ibid.*, p. 42.
[3] Gardiner, A. H., *The Theory of Proper Names*, London: Oxford Press, 1954, p. 30.

Gardiner observes that any words, including PNs, may be used in speech in various ways without deviation from the rules. He argues that in Speech, i.e., "the *ad hoc*, historically unique utilization of language may bend to its immediate purpose a word not constitutionally shaped to the use for which it is employed."

Thus we may use PNs as common-names, e.g., "the two Johns" or "Every country has its Babylon," "an academy," "a Ford."

"Sun" may be used as a common name and as a PN. "'The sun' is indeed potentially a general name, hence if any other entity except our own sun had the same qualities the same word *sun* would have to be used to denote it ... But *sun* would have become a proper name ... if we refuse it to give it to any other celestial body which resembles our sun in many respect." [1]

Now to argue correctly that PNs have meaning and that meaning is analogous to "exchange value" and that we may use a PN as a common name is important; however, this is not enough to know what kind of meaning PNs do have.

Gardiner is ready to answer this question. A proper name according to him is

a word or group of words which is recognized as having identification as its specific purpose, and which achieves, or tends to achieve that purpose by means of distinctive sound alone, without regard to any meaning possessed by the sound from the start, or acquired by it through association with the object or objects thereby identified. [2]

The emphasis on "sound" was meant to distinguish PNs from those names which their use connote attributes. This led Gardiner to make a strange statement, namely, "Proper names are identificatory marks recognizable not by the intellect, but by the sense." [3]

It also led him to a theory rejected by him at the outset of his book, namely that there are PNs which are so to speak "Pure."

Referring to a Swedish grammarian Noreen who contends that some names are not thoroughbred (vollblut) PNs as long as they are attributive, Gardiner writes, if so then, "A Mr. Ironmonger lose his name if he returned to the trade of his forefathers?".[4] Nonetheless, in the same book he makes use of the distinction between a Pure PN and Impure one.

[1] *Ibid.*, p. 37.
[2] *Ibid.*, p. 75.
[3] *Ibid.*, p. 40.
[4] *Ibid.*, p. 3.

He writes, "Names like John and Mary, Giovanni, Deauville, are less pure proper names because of the assistance that, on rare occasions they might give by their suggestion of sex, nationality or country." [1]

Pure PNs are defined as those which "are wholly arbitrary and totally without significance – unlike *Oxford* or *Mont Blanch*." According to Gardiner, signs like "Popocatepetl" and "Vercingeloria" strike us as wholly arbitrary" and therefore are mong the purest PNs since because of ignorance of their bearers we should feel no trace of meaning about them."

Gardiner admits that he cannot provide "a water-tight definition" for PN "since there are exact individually applied names which are not proper names, and commonly applied names which are."

For example, he takes surnames as names which are commonly applied and words like "moon" and "zero" to be individual names but not PNs. For this supposed difficulty alone he rejects his previous notion that PNs are individual names.

In my book on *Speech and Language* (P. 41), I wrongly defined a proper name as a word referring to a single individual. In this mistake, however, I am in good company, both the *Oxford English Dictionary* and Prof. Wyld's *Universal English Dictionary* share in the error.[2]

Let us evaluate some of Gardiner's statements.

First, Gardiner, unlike many logicians, recognizes that there are varieties of PNs. Any discussion of PNs at least warrants an indication that besides ordinary PNs such as "John" and "Mary" there are other names such as surnames, common names used as PNs. PNs used as common names, etc.

However, the use of a dichotomy of Language-Speech does not give us any added insight into the functions of PNs.

It is not clear at all when one should take a word as an item in speech and when as an item in language. A lexicographer who supposedly deals with words in language limits his research if he abandons the search for the usage of words in speech.

Taking Gardiner's example "sun" we shall see that in a *good* dictionary usually there are at least two entries under it, namely,

[1] *Ibid.*, p. 42.
[2] *Ibid.*, p. 29.

(1) "the star that is the central body of the solar system ..."
(2) "A self-luminous heavenly body ..." [1]

Thus we may say that "sun" is used both as a PN, i.e., to refer to our sun, and as a common name, i.e., to refer to any sun – without using the questionable speech-language dichotomy.

Second, Gardiner correctly takes "the identification" and "the individual application" of a PN as the silent feature of it. But then he assumes wrongly that surnames are "common proper names." Surnames, however, are not common names. A common name like "Human" is applicable to any being which has a set of specific properties. A surname is used to refer to any member of a group not in virtue of a set of its specific properties. There are specific properties belonging to humans, but there are no set of specific properties belonging to the Kennedys in virtue of which they are called by that name. In fact, neither the existence of "individually applied names which are not proper names" nor "commonly applied names which are" warrants rejection of his early theory which maintained that PNs are individual names.

Only a slight modification is needed to save the theory against these objections.

If we say, for example, that a PN *qua* PN is purported to be used to refer to an individual and never to refer to more than one individual, then we could argue that the use of a surname is not inconsistent with this statement. For a surname is used as an aid for the purpose of referring to an individual. If we call someone by using his first name and more than one person answers to it, we may add his surname (and if that won't help, a middle-name or a definite description or a demonstrative pronoun, if we have to) in order to make a correct identification possible.

Indeed surnames are invented in order to facilitate the unique referring act and not to hinder it.

Third, Gardiner's assertion that the purpose of identification is achieved by "distinctive sound alone, without regard to any meaning possessed by the sound" is absurd.

In fact, it violates his earlier assertion that PNs are words, i.e., "meaning-bearing sound." One consequence of this assertion is his naive epistemology that PNs "are recognizable not by the intellect but by the sense." A mere sound does not tell us at all

1 *The Random House Dictionary of the English Language.* 1966 Random House, Inc.

that it has a certain function, namely, it is designed to refer to a particular entity. Obviously, unless we know its functions we do not know that a sound is used as a PN.

Gardiner's motive is to defend a portion of Mill's theory that PNs denote but do not connote. This could be done by pointing out that we do not normally use a PN to convey information about its bearer to the hearer but to prepare the hearer that some information is forthcoming.

2. Sørensen

In his recent book *The Meaning of Proper Names* [1] the Danish linguist, Holger Steen Sørensen offers a definiens formula for PNs.

He first rejects various theories offered (mostly by logicians) about PNs.

He agrees with Gardiner that PNs are not mere noises, like the sounds produced by a car engine; rather they are meaning-bearing sounds, that is, words. And "Since we cannot know the meaning of a sign unless it has meaning" he argues "it follows that "Paris" has meaning. Similarly with other proper names ... but many people might not know its meaning."

He rejects, for obvious reasons, the view that a PN must have a denotation. Quoting Reichenbach's statement, viz., "A proper name is a symbol coordinated by definition to an individual thing. If a term is to be called a proper name it is necessary that there is a corresponding thing." He comments that if this statement is true "We must await the result of the investigation of the historians before we can class the sign S among proper names." But it is absurd to assume that the works of the historians have any bearing on linguistics or on logic.

Sørensen also tries to reject the assumption that PNs are arbitrary (Mill). He argues that those who assume this would probably believe also that "all signs, with the exception of onomatopoetic signs are arbitrary in the Saussurean Sense(s) of the word."

His second argument is that there are some rules which govern

---

[1] Sørensen, H. S., all references are to *The Meaning of Proper Names: With a Definiens Formula For Proper Names in Modern English*, Copenhagen: G.E.C. GAD Publisher, 1963.

naming, for example, "a child should have its father's surname."

Sørensen tries to provide a definition for PN after rejecting various theories by making use of the Speech-Language dichotomy. Strangely enough, he tries to do so while asserting that "'I' and 'you' are indefinable – they are semantic primitives of the English language."

A definition of PN is given as follows:

Let "P" be a variable for a proper name. And let "X" be a variable for an appellative stem + singular flexive. This, then, is the partial definition formula – and what is on the right-hand side of the equation mark the partial definiens formula-of proper name:

$$\text{"P"} = \text{"the X that } \ldots \text{"}$$

It follows, Sørensen argues, that a PN cannot possibly denote more than one entity.

He writes "From the fact that definiens of proper names contain, and begin with, the definite article and an appellative stem in the singular, it follows that proper names are individual names."

Now if a PN is identified with some properties of its denotation, then it could be argued that it is dispensable. Sørensen, in fact, draws this conclusion. Thus he writes:

In the case of proper names: theoretically we could do without them, but it is very inexpedient to have to say "the person that ...," therefore we say "Anderson," or whatever it may be.

He also argues that "Proper names are individual names in Language" whereas "'I,' 'your sister,' 'this hat,' ... are individual names in Speech: they denote one and only one entity on each occasion of their use (if they denote) ... isolated from the individual act of speech, ... these signs are general names, ... in Language."

However, being aware that a PN may denote different individuals he argues that:

It is an indisputable fact that proper names denote the same entity on different occasions of their use, or, in the case of two or more meanings, that, by the way of example, "Gaitskell$_1$" or ("Gaitskell" with meaning$_1$) always denotes Gaitskell$_1$, "Gaitskell$_2$" always Gaitskell$_2$.

To sum up, he writes:

From the fact that definiens of proper names contain, and begin with, the definite article and an appellative stem in singular, it follows that proper names are individual names; and from the fact that no Speech alternant is a constituent of their definiens, it follows that the individuality of proper names is not restricted to Speech. In other words: it follows that proper names are capable of denoting one and only one entity, in Language (and in Speech), in virtue of the structure of their meaning.[1]

The theory is open to the following criticism:

1. Despite the numerous warnings of recent logicians, Sørensen identifies the meaning of a PN with the statement expressing the unique description of its bearer. Strawson, commenting on this theory, observes that despite the fact the author "himself emphasized that identity of denotatum is no guarantee of identity of meaning and illustrated the point. He seems, ... to be committed to a contradiction: that a proper name, in so far as it stands for a single bearer, has both one meaning only and many more than one." [2]

2. Now consider that there may be many bearers of a name. In that case not only are there many descriptions of the same bearer, and therefore, upon his theory, many meanings of that name, but also there would be as many meanings of that name as there are bearers of that name.

3. I do not want to criticize the other defects in the theory such as the use of the dubious Speech-Language categories or the assumption that pronouns are indefinable, but only to show that his distinctions that some phrases – such as "Your sister" and "this hat" are general names in Language but individual names in Speech, whereas PNs are individual names in Language, stand on sand. As we had occasion to observe "sun" is used both as a PN and as a common name and such *usages* are also indicated in dictionaries which are supposed to be the depository of items of Language, i.e., words and not the depository of items of Speech. Likewise "John" may be used to refer to one and only one entity but not always, e.g., "John Doe." We use "John Doe," not as the name of anyone, (not even as an *ambiguous name* – despite the

---

[1] *Idem.*
[2] Strawson, P., "Review of Sørensen 'The Meaning of Proper Names'," *Mind*, volume LXXV, April, 1966, p. 298.

fact that it is used as such by some logicians, e.g., Suppes *Introduction to Logic*) but as a second order name, which encompasses every first-sur-name.

3. Syntactic Regularities

The interest of logicians is concentrated on those aspects of PNs which are supposed to be independent of the pecularities of any specific language. Only by way of examples are there references to PNs as they are used in English. Otherwise, their theories of PNs, if true, are intended to account for PNs in *any* language, or at least in languages having structural similarities.

On the other hand, linguists and descriptive grammarians, so far as they are interested in PNs, are concerned with establishing regularities which pertain to a specific language – in our case, the English language.

Although the syntactic aspects of PNs are parasitic upon more fundamental features, i.e., semantic and pragmatic, we shall not ignore the observations of some grammarians and some linguists even though they are only relevant to the English language.

Otto Jespersen, in his book *Essentials of English Grammar*, writes, "As a rule proper names need no article, as they are definite enough in themselves." He observes, however, that when a plural is formed of a PN the article is required because it ceases to be a PN "in the fullest sense," e.g., *the Stuarts*. "In accordance with this rule we have the article with geographical names with plural forms: *the West Indies, the Netherlands*, etc. Likewise, when we refer to members of a family the article is used with plural: *the Carlyles*." [1]

This rule, however, breaks down when we consider that some PNs are used with definite articles even though they are used in a singular form, e.g., *The Thames, The New York Times*. Chomsky suggests that such "Determiners" may be taken as part of the name itself. He writes:

Proper nouns are nouns with no Determiner (or, as in the case of "The Nile," with a fixed Determiner that may just as well be taken as part of the noun itself, rather than as part of a freely and independently selected Determiner system). [2]

[1] Jespersen, O., *Essentials of English Grammar*, London: George Allen, 1960, p. 205.
[2] *Ibid.*, p. 100.

If we accept this proposal we should also consider that there are "Determiners" which accompany some expressions used as PNs but could not be regarded as part of the expression itself. For example, the definite article as used in the following expressions is not a meaningless or decorative sign:

"The United States"

"The British Common-Wealth"

"The East German Democratic Republic"

"The Round Table"

(Witness here Strawson's observation on descriptions growing capital letters.)

Sørensen observes that, " 'The United States,' must, no doubt, be registered as an appellative construction: 'the' is a determinative; it is the definite article: 'The United States of *America*' (The use of capital letters is a convention of speech enconomy parallel to the use of capital latters in 'the Channel')." [1]

However, the distinction between PNs and definite descriptions and common names used as PNs is not clear cut. A PN could be used as a description and a definite description or a common name could be used as a PN. Hence we should not take the criterion of the absence of an article or a "Determiner" very seriously.

Consider how proper names such as "Quisling," "Pegasus" or "Chimaera" are now used as common nouns.

Partridge, in his book *Proper Names That Have Become Common Property*, writes [2]: "Quisling . . . had shed his capital letters with a speed unequalled by any of the several hundred other men . . . who have entered our dictionaries." Since Quisling was a famous traitor during the Second World War, the phrase "he is a quisling" meant "he is a traitor."

"The Chimaera" in Greek mythology was the name of a dragon-tailed, lion-headed, goat-bodied animal slain by Bellerophon as aided by the winged horse Pegasus. We now use "chimaera" to mean an idle fancy. In such cases PNs drop their definite articles and their capitals and take their place among other words.

---

[1] Sørensen, H. S., *Word-Classes in Modern English*, Copenhagen: GAD Publisher, 1958, p. 168.

[2] Patridge, E. R., *Name into Word: Proper Names That Have Become Common Property*, New York: The MacMillan Company, 1950, p. 356.

Consider also some contexts in which some typical PNs are used as common names. "This is just like Joan," "Here comes another Hitler," "This is not the Joan I married." In each case the PN is used not to refer to an individual but to refer to some properties of that individual.

On the other hand, we use some descriptions as PNs. Mill observed that "Dartmouth" is used as a name of a city. We may continue to use it as such, even if the river Dart changes its course. Such surnames as "Blond" (the fair), "Musard" (the dreamy), "Roger Deus Salvet Dominas" (Roger God-save-the-ladies) which were originally personal nicknames and given simply as description or in admiration or fun were recorded in *Domesday Book* (a sort of General Directory for 1086).[1]

We may use and apply the designation "The United States" to refer to our country even if the Federal Government absorbs all the political powers of every state. The appelation "The East German Democratic Republic" is used to refer to a part of Germany despite the fact that politically that state is neither democratic nor a republic.

In each case, if we need to indicate that we are using these expressions only as a PN and not as a description we may use the expression "the so-called."

The expression "The East German Democratic Republic," in fact, is often used by the West Germans with the prefix *"sogenannte"* to dispel the impression that the expression is a description. Lastly, consider Jesperson's observation with regard to the presence of a plural: that when on some rare occasions a plural is formed of a PN the article is required because it ceases to be a PN "in the fullest sense." No reason is given for this conviction. Perhaps the reason is this, that when we use *the Carlyles* (to announce the arrival of Mr. and Mrs.) or *the Alps* (to refer to groups of mountains in France and Italy) we use each name as a *group name*. However, this cannot be said about *The Netherlands* or *The United States*, since *The Netherlands* or *The United States* is not in number contrast with *the Netherland* or *an United State*.

To conclude, neither the absence of "the" nor the plural sign ("S") could be regarded as criteria for signs used as PNs.

1 Mathews, C. M., *English Surnames*, Weidenfeld and Nicholson. 1966, p. 32.

Another criterion for an expression used as a PN in English is that, in general, such expressions are capitalized.

Gardiner, however, observes that there are expressions such as "Thursday" and "January" which are not properly speaking PNs, though they are capitalized.

No doubt many expressions are capitalized which are not usually regarded to be PNs such as the names of days, months, institutions, and a variety of others such as "Ten Command-ments," "Coca-Cola," "the Pope."

However, before we pass judgment on such expressions and regard them as exceptions to the rule, we have to decide whether they are uniquely referring expressions used for identification of a particular entity *qua* particular, i.e., PNs, or whether they are used as expressions which are used to refer to a type of things, i.e., common names.

As a reminder, let us note that in many languages there are no capital letters or signs for the definite article either.

By now it should be evident that a purely syntactic approach is not conducive to clear understanding of the pragmatic and semantic aspects of PNs. Rather the syntactic side of the issue is the offshoot of the other dimension. That is, unless we settle what function or functions PNs have in language and what significant relation, if any, does exist between certain kinds of expressions and some extra-linguistic entities, the miscellaneous grammatical facts pertaining to a specific language are of secondary import.

Using Wittgenstein's expression, we suggest that "the surface grammar" is not enough. We need a "depth grammar" in order to get hold of the concept of names.

IV. A CONSTRUCTIVE MOVE

We have had occasion to observe how often logicians, linguists and grammarians have propounded all too-simple theories concerning the seemingly simple problem: What is in a name?

Pertaining to the semantic dimension of PNs it has been said, as we observed, that they are meaningless signs – they are words and hence meaning-bearing signs – they are denotative but not connotative signs – they have both sense and in most cases denotation – they are individual names – they are replaceable by the definite description – they are items of *Language* and not of *Speech*.[1]

Pertaining to the syntactic dimension it has been argued that certain kind of structures, e.g., the absence of Determiners and plural signs or the presence of capital letters, do uniquely determine, at least in English, whether an expression is a PN.

In all these arguments, it is presupposed that the class of PNs is a well-defined class, hence theories were offered concerning the properties of the members of this class with the intention of differentiating them from other expressions such as common names, descriptive phrases, pronouns. This presupposition, at least, stands in need of examination.

---

[1] Note, for example the following: "It is a mistake to think that 'referring expression' itself can secure and guarantee this uniqueness. This is obvious in the case of proper names, for here we cannot appeal to meaning. 'Tommy Jones' does not have a meaning, and many people share it. Proper names are usually (rather) common names." Linskey, L., *Referring*, London: Routledge & Kegan Paul, 1967, p. 118.

1. On Dictionary Definition

> Do not say: 'There *must* be something common' ...
> but *look* and *see*...
>
> *Philosophical Investigations*

It seems *prima facie* that there is no problem in knowing what a PN is. A *good* dictionary may easily provide us with the required information.

Consulting a *good* dictionary we find, for example, the following under PN:

A noun which is not normally preceded by an article or other limiting modifier, as *any some* and that refers to only one person or thing or to several persons or things which constitute a unique class only because they have the same name, as *Lincoln, Pittsburgh*.[1]

This definition is only of limited value. We have observed that *any* expression and not only *a noun* may be used as a PN. That some of these expressions carry with themselves modifiers as a part of the name, and some carry modifiers as a sign of the definite description. The modifying clause of the above definition that a noun may refer "to several persons or things which constitute a unique class only because they have the same name" is not helpful at all. I wonder what constitutes a unique class without having some property except having the same name! I suppose this is intended to take care of surnames. But a surname is not a class name. It is only an auxiliary expression which may make identification easier in cases when the use of a first name fails to achieve its purpose. And this happens when many persons have the same first or perhaps same middle name. For centuries in European countries individuals were distinguished by their Christian names only. And some churches still ignore surnames. However, as a result of the increase in population and, perhaps, some other factors such as greater need for identification in our complex civilization, it became necessary to employ some further expressions by which one individual might be distinguished from others. Were a person conspicuous enough there would be no need for a surname or a middle name. Thus in England the royal family sign by their baptismal names only.

The dictionary characterization of PN as referring (apart to a

---

[1] *Idem. The Random House Dictionary of the English Language*, under "Proper Noun."

thing also) to a unique class only in virtue of having the same name, in effect, would fit the description of common names from the nominalistic point of view. Since, according to a traditional view of nominalists, the only things which the members of *any* class have in common are names, e.g., Hobbes writes "things which are called by one name have only their name in common." This, I think, is enough to show that the information given in dictionaries is hopelessly inadequate. The only part of the definition which may be regarded as true is the statement that PNs "refer to only one person or thing" and that needs a great amount of clarification.

Obviously, one should not expect to learn a great deal about PNs by consulting a good dictionary. No entry under a PN is a substitute for a book on this topic. However, a dictionary at least should not mislead its readers as it does in this case.

That the dictionary, by itself, is not the highest court of appeal may be substantiated not only by finding mistakes in it, but by remembering how dictionaries are compiled.

As an empirical investigator, a lexicographer is supposed to report certain regularities pertaining to the use of certain types of expressions in a certain natural language. These regularities are then organized and constituted as entries under certain expressions. In organizing the entries a lexicographer employs various concepts borrowed from various fields such as grammar, philosophy, linguistic, etc. However, there is no reason to assume that these concepts are clear enough to be useful or that the lexicographers make a correct use of them.

In order to support this thesis we need not bother with the way various sophisticated concepts such as Number, Cause, Intention, Motive, etc. are defined in dictionaries but only observe various entries under the seemingly unproblematic concept as PNs.

Gardiner, as we observed, claimed that he was misled by entries given under PNs in some excellent dictionaries. Notice that the admitted mistake is a mistake in classifying PN as an expression referring to a single individual. The more serious problem, i.e., what is an "individual" or what is not an individual or not a particular, (for example, a universal), is not even raised.

The problem will manifest itself by taking a cursory glance at the following list in which various expressions, which are generally

PROPER NAMES

A
Personal Names

1. First-Middle-Sur-Name
2. Patronym
   * "Macdonald" (Son of Donald)
3. Cognomen
   "Cicero"
4. Pen-Name
5. Nick-Name *
6. Mythical-Name
   * "Zeus" "God"
7. Fictitious-Name
   "Pickwick" * "John Doe" ***
8. By-Name (surname, but not family name)

B
Place Names

1. Geo-political
   "The United States" "The Netherlands"
   "The East-German-Democratic-Republic"
2. City – District – States Names
3. Geographical-Names
   "The Thames" "The Equator"
   "Mont Blanch" "Dora" (hurricane's name)
4. Astronomical-Name
   "The Universe" "Moon"
   "The Pleiades" (a name for a cluster of stars)
5. Fictitious-Name "Yoknapatawpha"

* Used also as description
** Used also as a common name
*** Is the second order name, which covers every first-surname.

C
Time Names

1. Historical-Names
   "The Glorious Revolution" *
   "The Twentieth Century" *
2. Periods
   "Winter", "Monday" **
   "Dooms Day" * "Easter" **

D
Institution Names

1. Political
   "Parliament" "The French Academy" **
   "The Communist Party" **
   "The Supreme Court" **
2. Economic
   "General Motors" "Coca-Cola" **

E
Artifact Names

1. Artistic Products
   "The Eroica" **
   "Venus de Milo"
   "Mickey Mouse" **
   "Hamlet" **
2. Cultural items
   "Tractatus Logico-
   Philosophicus" **
   "Barborosa" (war-plan)
3. Numerals
   "one" **
4. Mythical
   "The Argo" (a mythical
   ship) "Excalibur"
   (the magic sword of
   King Arthur)

regarded as falling under category of PN, appear. Provisionally I
divid PN into five categories of:

A. Personal Names
B. Place Names
C. Time Names
D. Institution Names
E. Artifact Names

Each category is divided into many sub-categories and an
example is provided for some unfamiliar cases. (Notice that some
names fall under various sub-categories.)

My main purpose in providing this list is to show that even a
simple list of PNs is enough to vitiate the simple-minded definitions which we find in dictionaries, grammars, logical treatises
and even in the works of linguists.

I suggest, therefore, that we leave dictionaries, grammars, etc.,
alone and try to find out for ourselves what a PN is.

2. *The Pragmatic Dimension*

> The notion or definition of a house would be as follows:
> a shelter to protect us from harm by wind or rain or
> scorching heat; while another will describe it as stones,
> bricks and timbers.
>
> Aristotle *De Anima*

In the rest of this work I will try to bring out some positive
features of PNs. We may be able to find an answer to our
question if, instead of pursuing a semantic inquiry, i.e., search for
a supposed relation between words and things, or a syntactic
inquiry, i.e., inquiry into relations of expressions, we take a close
look at pragmatics, namely, an inquiry into the relations between
expressions and the users of expressions.

The inquiry into the pragmatic dimension should precede the
semantic and syntactic and not vice versa, as it is often done by
logicians and grammarians. That is, unless we find out first the
kinds of expressions which are used by speakers of a language for
achieving a certain end we should not cut out the speaker and his
needs from the picture and look at language as something
possessing, by itself, certain internal or external properties.

My suggestion that the inquiry into pragmatics should precede
that of other dimensions is not based alone on observing the

inadequacies of such alternative approaches, but is also grounded on the fact that the use of this approach is conducive to clarity and would create fewer problems.

Let us illustrate this point. Suppose we define "tool" as any object possessing specified physical properties on the ground that a "tool" does in fact denote various objects, each possessing certain physical properties. We have now created for ourselves a problem of redefining our definiendum each time we invent a new tool. More seriously, in investigating a newly discovered civilization or prehistoric cultures we would exclude from the list of tools any object not resembling physically our tools.

On the other hand, if we consider the pragmatic dimension by looking first at certain human needs, motives and goals, and then finding that certain artifacts or even natural objects (no matter what physical properties they may have) are instrumental in fulfilling these needs, motives and goals, then we would not have to face the aforementioned problems. Under the new definition, any object, and it need not be a physical object, which is used in order to satisfy certain needs, motives and goals, may be counted as a "tool." We may say, taking a hint from Aristotle, that in defining an artifact, such as a tool or a house or an artificial body, such as a court or a corporation, the purpose for which each artifact or each artificial body is made should be included in the definiens, since an artifact or an artificial body is not a mere assemblage but a purposeful configuration of objects, persons, etc.

Let us now make use of the tool analogy and look at language as a kind of a tool used to satisfy primarily social needs. (Don't balk at dissimilarities. An analogy is not a proof.)

Making allowances for some very primitive and pre-historic societies, it may be said that primarily language is employed by men to convey information, evaluations, and recommendations. It is used secondarily also for numerous other ends, such as counting, warning, contracting, swearing, singing and soliloquizing, etc.

Corresponding to each activity we make use of a certain type of linguistic expression. For example, to convey information, we do make statements (that is we make use of sentences which have truth-value); for recommending we make use of prescriptive utterances; for counting we make use of numerals.

3. The Need for Identification

> God needeth not to distinguish his Celestiall servants
> by names.
>
> Hobbes, *Leviathan* III, XXXIV, 213.

Now, in order that we satisfy the need to identify uniquely various
entities, but not to identify them *qua* their types, and, once
having uniquely identified them, in order to refer to these entities
or distinguish them from others, we make use of certain kinds of
expressions. Following Strawson we may call them "uniquely
referring expressions."

It might be objected, at this very point, that the assumption of
the existence of certain universal needs is *a priori*. There is no
reason to assume, for example, that men do need to identify
various objects and make unique reference to persons, places,
artifacts, segments of time, etc.

This objection is captious. Not only can there be no histories,
geographies, biographies, novels, myths, etc., but more basically
there can be no family relations, tribal institutions, or political
organizations, even at the most primitive level without the
existence of some linguistic expressions by means of which
significant persons, places, times and objects are uniquely
identified and referred to.

Such "necessities" and "impossibilities" are *post factum* and
hence not *a priori*. That is, they are essential constituents of
institutional facts. No doubt there were and still are societies for
which sub-categories of time are of no importance – years and
seasons, perhaps, but not hours, minutes and seconds. For others,
however, time is gold and every fleck of it counts. Hence a device,
i.e., a chronometer is used for giving names to a number of brief
events.

No one, of course, ought to have the similar kind of interest or
the same sort of device for attaining his ends as others. But do we
know of any one for whom no particular person or place or time
or institution is of some interest?

The world in which things are nameless is a strange world.
Alice, *Through The Looking Glass* is momentarily confronted with
such a world: "This must be the wood," she said thoughtfully to
herself, "where things have no names. I wonder what'll become of
my name when I go in? I shouldn't like to lose it at all – because

they'd have to give me another, and it would be almost certain to be an ugly one."

4. Referring Expressions

Given the fact that speakers of a language are interested in identifying, referring and distinguishing uniqeuly the identity of a referent, no matter what kind of a referent, we can discover the types of expressions which are used to achieve these ends.

If we look at the English language we can find at least four kinds of uniquely referring expressions. These are, according to Strawson:

1. Singular demonstrative pronouns
2. Singular personal and impersonal pronouns
3. Definite descriptions
4. Proper Names

Although singular demonstrative pronouns, singular personal and impersonal pronouns and definite descriptions are all referring expressions, they do differ from PNs in achieving this function in different ways.

Pronouns such as "this," "that," "it," "I," "he," "she," "you" are used referringly by different speakers to denote different entities on different occasions of their uses.

This difference is enough to mark them off from definite descriptions and proper names.

Note that we may use a definite description or even a PN to refer uniquely to various referents, but in all these cases we are able to reinforce the role of an expression so that we clearly individuate the referent. We may use for example, "The king of France" to refer to various French kings, "The Twentieth Century" as a name for a segment of time not beginning with the Birth of Christ, "London" to refer to London, Ontario, and "Joan" to refer to many women. But in each case such anomalies may be prevented by using other expressions such as adding a sur-name, middle-name to the first name, saying "my Joan and not your Joan," "The king of France who was guillotined."

Thus both definite descriptions (the forms "The So and So") and PNs may be used to refer to various persons or things; however, they always *purport*, in any particular context, to name only one entity.

Jespersen alludes to the fact that a PN may name many persons but nevertheless its use presupposes naming only one individual.

A more serious difficulty encounters us when we reflect that *John* and *Smith* by common consent are reckoned among proper names, and yet it is indubitable that there are many individuals that are called *John*, and many that are called *Smith* ... What in my view is of prime importance is the way in which names are actually employed by speakers and understood by hearers. Now, every time a proper name is used in actual speech its value to both speaker and hearer is that of denoting one individual only, and being restricted to that one definite being.[1]

5. PNs and Definite Descriptions

It seems now that there is a close affinity between an expression used as the definite description and an expression used as PN, since both types may be used by different speakers to refer uniquely to the same entity throughout on different occasions of their uses. "Winston Churchill" and "The Prime Minister of England during 1940–45" are used by different speakers to refer to one and only one man, whenever they are used referringly.

However, as we have noted before, PN and the definite description may not be used interchangeably – except in certain contexts.

What distinguishes PNs from definite descriptions is the fact noted by Wittgenstein that naming is not describing but only a preparation for description. Or to use a simile, a PN is a peg on which we hang descriptions, but it is not in itself replaceable by the definite description. However, a PN may be used as a description and hence may lose its status as a PN.

That is, if we take "Zeus" to mean "The supreme deity of the ancient Greeks" then we impose upon it a truth-value and a truth-value is a property of a definite description, but not a property of a PN unless a PN, in virtue of its association with its bearer, absorbs some of its properties and so turns into a definite description. Notice the case when we use a wrong name. If I refer to the present Prime Minister of England (in 1967) by using "Churchill" I have committed a mistake of not knowing some descriptions which fall under that name.

---

[1] Jespersen, O., *The Philosophy of Grammar*, London: Allen and Unwin, 1924, p. 65.

6. Identifying – Referring and Distinguishing

The three facets of PN, namely the identifying, referring and distinguishing uses, are closely related, though distinct. Using a PN one may simultaneously achieve all three acts, but also one may want to achieve only one.

If I have had occasion to point to someone and say, "this is Winston Churchill," then I am referring to a man who has done some astonishing things. At the same time I am identifying him if I want to distinguish him from some other people around him. But if I say, "I want to be Churchill" or "Who is Churchill?" or "Churchill rhymes with . . ." or "Churchill is mortal or Churchill is not mortal," I am neither referring to the famous Prime Minister nor identifying him nor distinguishing him. Though in the first and the second case I used his name, in the third case I mentioned his name and in the fourth case I used his name vacuously.

This shows that PNs, like other expressions, may be used for ends other than their normal functions, though there are no sharp boundaries between normal and non-normal functions.

7. The Referent

In exhibiting the various functions of a PN, we need not commit ourselves to the ontological status which the referent of the PN may have. The fact that the referents of some PNs are spatio-temporal entities or characters in plays and novels or heroes and gods in myths, is irrelevant. Indeed, "To give to airy nothing a local habitation and a name" to quote Shakespeare, is the occupational disease of the poets. However, preoccupation with the status of the referent of some PNs led some logicians to fabricate myths about PNs, rather than describe their nature.

For example Quine writes that:

There is a tendency to try to preserve some shadowy entity under the word 'Cerberus,' for example, lest the word lose its meaning. If 'Cerberus' were meaningless, not only would poetry suffer, but even certain blunt statements of fact, such as there is no such thing as Cerberus would lapse into meaningless . . . 'Cerberus' remains meaningful despite not naming . . . Some meaningful words which are proper names from a grammatical point of view, notably 'Cerberus' do not name anything.[1]

[1] *Ibid.*, p. 199–202.

This suggests that an expression, in order to be a genuine name, should name something in *rebus naturae*.

"Cerberus," however, names something, i.e., the three-headed dog which guarded the infernal regions, according to the classic mythology.

There is no reason to assume that PNs should denote spatio-temporal entities. Nothing prevents "Zorotaster" from being a name, even if there never was a man by that name, except a prejudice that every PN has to be a name of some region of space-time.

The same may be said about other referring expressions. Consider the fact that referring expressions such as "this" and "that," "I" and "thou" are used in religious discourse or fictions to refer uniquely to entities which are not necessarily spatio-temporal.

Likewise, expressions such as "the average man," "the un-conscious motive," "the ideal gas" are used by scientists as referring expressions, though in virtue of being formal concepts of a model, do not have observable phenomena as their referents.

The link between PNs and their supposed bearers is tenuous. A PN does not lose its meaning if its bearer (if it has a bearer) goes out of existence. In this respect PNs are like common names.

8. Overlapping Categories

Not every referring expression is used to individuate a unique referent. If I say, "Have a coke," any liquid which falls under the description of being a Coca-Cola will do. (In fact, legally speaking nothing could be a Coca-Cola unless it has certain specific de-scriptions – among them the fact that it is manufactured by that company alone.)

Hence, it seems that such names which usually fall under the categories of E and D, that is, some names of Artifacts, or Insti-tutions, in virtue of the fact that many items may fall under them *qua* palpable resemblances would be regarded, at least sometimes, as common names. Since there are many copies of "The Holy Bible," many renditions of "The Eroica," many copies of "The New York Times," many cartoons of "Mickey Mouse" (not to speak of mickey mouse democracies) and even many interpretations of "Hamlet," the name of such objects may be regarded as a common name.

On the other hand, we may say unless a perfect replica of the Mona Lisa or Venus De Milo is produced, their names are used as PNs.

However, if we say not "anything which does have instances" but "anything which may have instances *qua* having certain properties" is not a unique entity, but rather a type of thing, and hence its name is a common name, then we would destroy the traditional distinction between common names and proper names which correspond to the metaphysical categories of universals and particulars. There is nothing sacrosanct about traditional categories. We may look at any universal as a particular and at any particular as a universal. The existence of such categories is to be justified on pragmatic grounds.

But since, as a matter of fact, we are interested in identifying uniquely persons and things, we need PNs. That is not to say that a PN may not be used as a common name or a common name as a PN. Only by observing how an expression is used may we determine whether it is used as a PN or a common name.

The temptation, however, to reduce PNs to common names or common names to PNs is very strong (or metaphysically speaking to reduce particulars to universals or universals to particulars).

Kneale, in line with Frege, takes numerals to be PNs of numbers. He writes, "When the word 'four' is used as a noun, e.g., in the statement 'four is an even number,' it seems to behave as Frege says, like a proper name."

For "2 + 2" and "4" are both used to refer to numbers. They are indeed proper names of a number, but names with different senses ... a proper name (which may be a single word or sign or a combination of such) *expresses* its sense, *but stands for* or *designates* its reference.[1]

The argument rests on Frege's assumption that every PN has a sense. But this, as we argued before, is to confine the function of a PN with the properties of its bearer.

Numerals are indeed names of numbers, but they are more like common names than simple PNs (though following Mill a distinction could be made between *singular collective name*, or a

---

[1] *Ibid.*, p. 495–496.

proper name of a class and a common name). The numeral "two" or "2" or "II" all are the names of the class of all couples and any set having the property of being a couple is entitled to this designation.

Indeed Frege did classify numerals with PNs, despite their dissimilarities. Frege writes:

> When we speak of "the number one" we indicate by means of the definite article a definite and unique object of scientific study. There are not diverse numbers one, but only one. In 1 we have a proper name, which as such does not admit of a plural any more than "Frederick the Great" or "the chemical element gold." [1]

This assumption rests on Frege's theory that a PN does have a sense and may have a denotation (which, in fact, vitiates the traditional distinction between PN and common name.)

Obviously neither "the one" nor "Frederick the Great "nor "the color black" admit of plurals. They are all using the grammarians' category may be called "individual names." However, not every individual name is a PN.

"Frederick the Great" unlike "the one" or "the black" does not have a sense (though once had a bearer) and for this very reason there are no instances of its bearer. Since there is no such property as Frederickness, there could be no instantiation of that property. On the other hand, every entity could be counted as one and many things are black, since there is something called "oneness" and another thing called "blackness."

To call numerals PNs is misleading not only because each numeral is a name of a number *qua* a definite property of that number, but also because, unlike PNs, numerals are not assigned to entities by an *ad hoc* convention.

9. *A Use – Mention Confusion*

One possible explanation for taking a PN as a common name and hence asking for its meaning is the way PNs find their way into our dictionaries. In ordinary dictionaries the names of some significant persons and places appear among other words. The

[1] Frege, *The Foundations of Arithmetic*, translated by J. L. Austin, Basil Blackwell, 1950, p. 49.

entries under these names provide some important descriptions of the bearers of the names.

This may induce us to believe that the meaning of a PN is the defeniens appearing under it, in the same way that the meanings of other words appear in the entries under them. Nonetheless, this belief is a mistake. The dictionary does not provide meaning for PNs nor defeniens for them, but only gives descriptions of the bearers of some PNs. Dictionaries do not tell us what the word "John" means in English, but do tell us who was John if John was "somebody." However, the confusion between use and mention in dictionaries and the appearance of PNs among other words delude us into thinking that dictionaries provide meaning for PNs.

Note, for example, the two entries under *Julian,* namely "Roman emperor 361–363" and "a boy's given name." [1] Julian was the Roman emperor; however, "Julian" is a boy's given name and also the name of that emperor. A name is not the emperor or an emperor a name.

10. Transformation to Common Names

PNs transform into common names if they absorb some properties of their bearers in virtue of their association. Thus "Quisling" became a common name in virtue of a notable description of Quisling. Likewise "Pegasus," "Gabriel" or "Ford" are also used as common names after absorbing some notable properties of their bearers. I may both say, "I have met Mr. Ford," and also "I don't want to buy a Ford," and "In no zoo may you find a Pegasus" or "Pegasus is the winged horse sprung from Medusa."

In these examples I used an expression both as a PN, i.e., the name of a particular entity, and a common name, i.e., the name of a type of things. Walt Disney bestowed the name "Mickey Mouse" on his major cartoon character and not on his pet mouse. In so doing the name stood for a type of a movie cartoon and not for a unique entity, so much so that later the term was used as an adjective, connoting artificiality, or lack of seriousness.

---

[1] Withycombe, *Idem.*

11. *The Protean Use of PN*

The use of a PN, both as making a unique reference to its bearer
and as a description of the properties of its bearer, fosters puzzles
and puns. Consider, "Here is another Hitler," "But there cannot
be another Hitler."

In Arabic, among the thousand names for God, is the descriptive phrase "The Necessary Being" (Vajēb-ál-Vojod). It is
then argued trivially that "The Necessary Being does exist" and
paradoxically that "The Necessary Being does not exist." Again
the question, "Is the Glorious Revolution glorious?" may be
taken both as trivial or a serious question.

In all these cases if clarity is desired we may make a distinction
between a PN and the properties of its bearer by using "so
called" or the like, reminding our hearers that we are using the
expression only as PN or only as properties of its bearer, e.g.,
"The so-called 'Glorious Revolution'," "The so-called 'Necessary-
Being'," or "He acts like Hitler," instead of "Here is another
Hitler."

The context in general may determine whether a PN is used as
a name or as a description, or is used vacuously or essentially or is
mentioned. If I say "Socrates was the teacher of Plato," I used
"Socrates" and "Plato" as proper names and I used both
expressions essentially since the statement would turn to falsehood by replacing "Plato" for "Socrates." But if I say "Socrates'
age plus Plato's equals Plato's age plus Socrates'," I am using
their names vacuously since the statement remains true by the
replacement of other expressions for "Socrates" or "Plato."
Indeed, in the latter case, I am not using either name as a PN but
only as substituents for variables in a skeleton of a mathematical
truth.

But if I say "'Socrates' is a proper name and not a description,"
I am using "Socrates" in order to mention his name and make some
grammatical point about it. Notice also that in limericks PNs are
used not to refer to a particular person or place (except acci-
dentally). In this respect names in limericks function like variables in logic, though their phonetic features are of some significance. Thus in "There was an old fellow called Brown ..." or
"There was an old man of Cape Horn – who wished he had never

been born," the names "Brown" and "Cape Horn" are used not to refer to any particular person or place. Other names may be used in their place without a loss.

The moral to be drawn is that PNs, like other linguistic expressions, are used for various ends. Nonetheless, we may avoid ambiguity and perhaps a tragedy by paying attention to the function of a PN, not only to its surface grammar. It is not the grammatical form of an expression which determines that an expression is a PN, but only the function which is assigned to that expression.

12. Same Person – Same Name

Since a PN is mostly used for referring uniquely to an entity and individuating it, it is necessary that it always be applied to the same entity. There are, however, various criteria for establishing whether a referent of a PN, e.g., a person, a city, a book, a portion of time, or an institution is *the same*. Examples of such criteria are spatio-temporal continuity, finger prints, answering to the name, temporal properties. Consider various criteria we use in order to establish that "He is the same man," "This is the same day," "This is the same army," "This is the same French Academy," "This is the same hurricane."

Without an appeal to a criterion we cannot know that a referent of a PN is the same or not. The same is true about the name itself. That is, in the absence of a criterion, we are unable to know whether a certain configuration of letters should be construed as *the same name*. According to some legal rules, the criterion that "X is the same PN as Y" is having the same sound and not necessarily the same spelling. This criterion is called *"Idem Sonans."* In a case when the identity of the beneficiary is in doubt, a name which sounds like another is considered to be the same, despite variance in spelling.[1]

The point is that in order to establish whether the bearers of a name are the same or whether names are the same we need to appeal to certain criteria.

Though a PN should always be applied to the *same* item, the converse is not the case. For persons, places, artifacts, etc., may

[1] Greene, L. G., *Law of Names*, New York: Oceana Publications, 1954.

have various names during their life span. Consider "Dr. Jekyll" and "Mr. Hyde," the names of the same person or "Everest" and "Gaurisanker," the names of the same mountain from opposite points of view.

13. Name-Givers

Using an expression as a PN presupposes that that expression was bequeathed by someone – e.g., parents, states, or authors, upon some bearer, e.g., infants, cities, books, ships, etc. – as a name so that if we want, we could refer to its bearer.

In this we should agree with Mill that pointing to a man and saying "Smith" or to a city and saying "London" we do not convey to the hearer any information except that these are their names.

Now giving a PN to an item presupposes that the name-giver is interested in the bearer *cum* individual and not necessarily *cum* its types.

Gardiner observes that "there is no human being so wretched as to have no name of his own" which, if true, shows that at least everyone has someone's interest.

It is reported that the Roman slaves originally were without names. Only after being sold they took their master's praenomen in the genitive case followed by the suffix – "por." (Boy), e.g., "Marcipor," which indicates that some men, so long as they were regarded by others as cattle, did not need a name. However, as soon as they became servants some designation was called forth.

14. Why Name?

"What's the use of their having names," the Gnat said, "if they won't answer to them?" "No use to *them*," said Alice, "but it's useful to the people that name them, I suppose. If not, why do things have names at all?"

Unless we are sufficiently interested in an item, and not *qua* its type, we do not bestow a name upon it. We do not give a name to any patch of cloud, but if the cloud turns into a hurricane, it might receive a name, e.g., "Dora."

Indeed, for a long time no one showed any interest even in

types of clouds until Luke Howard classified clouds under the names "Cumulus," "Cirrus" and "Stratus." Thus, by giving a form to recalcitrant matter it is made an object of inquiry.

We may say that if some item has a PN, then it indicates that some one was interested enough in that item to bestow upon it a name so that one may refer to it later. In general, we need PNs if we want to refer to the bearers of the name in their absence. Otherwise, pronouns would suffice.

The type of PNs given to persons and things may indicate something about the intention of the name-givers. Names such as *Ashes, Tribulation, The Lord is near, Praise-God Barebones,* and *if-Christ-had-not-died-for you-you-had-been-damned-Barebones,* (luckily shortened as *Damned Barebones*) were given by Puritans to their infants.[1] Hawthorne, by giving names as "Dimmesdale" or "Pearl" to two of his characters, prepares his readers to expect certain behavior befitting such names. This is not a mere inferance from the meaning of such names or from the properties of their bearers. In a passage in *The Scarlet Letter.* Hester, the heroin addressing Dimmesdale pleads "Do anything, save to lie down and die! Give up this name of Arthur Dimmesdale, and make thyself another, and a high one, such as thou canst wear without fear or shame." Some writers, like some parents, choose names for their characters because of their laudatory meaning (*Ernest*), derogatory connotation (*Murdstone,* Dickens), symbolic significance (*Godet*), or even just a sound (*Lulu*).

Where belief in magic of names is strong, parents uniformly give *good* names to their infants and seldom a *neutral* name and perhaps never a *bad* name.

According to Withycombe, "Foundlings were obvious subjects for the ingenuity of Puritan ministers, and they were freely given such names as *Helpless, Lament, Misericordia, Adulterina,*" [2] which shows what kind of being were these Puritans! To give a dog a bad name and hang him is to succumb to superstition and prejudice. You will not make your children good either by giving them good names. Hitherto I have spoken on the pragmatics of names only from the speakers' and, not from the hearers' point of

---

[1] Bowman, W. D., *The Story of Surnames,* p. 91.
[2] *Ibid.,* p. XXXIII.

view. Other interesting problems, such as the effect of names on their bearers, the reaction of the bearers to their names, the loss of ones names or others and the reasons behind it are relegated to the social psychologists.

15. Conventions

There are *ad hoc* conventions for bequeathing PNs to various things. There are, however, no general rules governing such activities. For this very reason, one is not entitled to draw inferences from a name about its bearer.

Here are a few examples of special conventions pertaining to the use of some PNs.

Children must bear the surnames of their fathers. Wives must bear the names of their husbands. "The old common law merged the personality of the wife with that of her husband ... as if wife lost her existence (legally) when she entered into a marriage." [1] Certain first names are usually given to males and others to females. The laws of some states prohibit a corporation from using a name already used by other corporations. No obscene word should be bestowed as a PN. According to a Revolutionary Law in France first names ought to be chosen only from the list of ancient names.

Since the use of PNs (unless regulated by some customs or laws) are arbitrary, one may easily change his name. Under the common law an individual may lawfully adopt any name without any legal proceedings unless it is done for a fraudulent purpose, e.g., imposture. We shall note that family names are not copyrighted. However, there are special regulations for the change of the name of a corporation or for assigning a fictitious name to it.

It is possible to adopt a more rational system for assigning personal names, for example, replacing systematically numerals and latters in place of first names and surnames – a kind of zip code for persons.

This would facilitate our present but defective method of identification by using names. It also would enable us to deduce some facts about the bearers of the names without knowing them. If this were to happen PNs like numerals might beget both sense and denotation.

[1] Greene, p. 54.

16. Problems of Translation

PNs, as such I argued, are not translatable and so we may look at them as an international item which belong to no specific language. That is not to say that they are not transliterated, i.e., rendered into a corresponding alphabet.

If a PN is used not only as a referring expression which identifies uniquely its bearer, but also as an expression which is intended to say something about its bearer, then the translator should translate those expressions. Thus, some nick-names such as "Shorty" (but not "Bobby"), some transparent names of novels such as "Great Expectations" (but not "Ulysses") if used as descriptions should be translated.

However, we should not worry about PNs which are now used purely as identification marks even though originally they were meant to be descriptions.

Thus we need not translate "Stuarts" even though once used as a description (stywards) – tending the king's pigs; "Johnson," even though at one time used as John's son (patronym); or "Plato," even though it was bestowed upon the great philosopher by his gymnastic master as a nick name meaning "broad." [1]

In novels and poems sometimes PNs are bestowed upon things for some specific reasons other than identification. Even the mere sound of a name is sometimes significant (for example, in rhyme) and hence, a good translator should transmit these significant concommitants of the names. Otherwise the reader may miss the point intended by the writer.

Thus, The name "Khayyam" is not translated, and need not be, when the name appears as a designation for the famous Persian poet. However, in this quatrain

> "Khayyam, who stitched the tents of science,
> Has fallen in griefs' furnace and been suddenly burned,
> The shears of Fate have cut the tent ropes of his life,
> And the broker of Hope has sold him for nothing!"

where Khayyam makes use of his name both as a name and description, that is, where he makes a pun on his name, translation

---

[1] Withycombe, *Idem.*

is necessary. Here it should be mentioned that "Khayyam" means "tent-maker" (which was his poetical name or *Takhallus*, adopted by the poet, perhaps because of his trade or his hereditary calling) as it is indeed mentioned by his famous translator Edward Fitzgerald.

Shakespeare in *A Midsummer – Night's Dream*, bestows charming names, for the sake of connotation and sound such as "Peaseblossom," "Mustardseed," "Moth," upon fairies.

In *King Henry IV, the Second Part*, to mock the wisdom of the crowd he gives such names as "Shallow," and "Silence" to country justices and "Mouldy" and "Shadow" to recruits.

This enables Falstaff to say "I do see the bottom of Justice Shallow" and Shallow to announce "Ha, ha, ha! most excellent, in faith! Things that are mouldy lack use" (Act III, Sc. II).

To convey the intention of the poet in giving such names to his characters and to show the puns made on names, all such proper names should be translated.

V. CONCLUSION

The concept of name and to a lesser degree that of proper name, despite the latter's apparent simplicity, has puzzled philosophers ever since the birth of philosophy. So that even in our time a famous logician complains that, "There is not yet a theory of the meaning of proper names upon which general agreement has been reached as the best." (Alonzo Church, *Introduction to Mathematical Logic*) More recently a philosopher asks; "Do they (proper names) have sense in the same way that adjectives, common nouns, and definite descriptions have sense! In the history of philosophy answers to this question have been crucial to answering the general question of how words relate to the world." (John Searle, "Proper Names And Descriptions" *The Encyclopedia of Philosophy*).

In ancient times the interest of philosophers in common and proper names was subordinated to their metaphysical concern with such things as universals and particulars which are supposed to provide denotata for sematico-grammatical categoris of common and proper names. Common names are taken to name a universal, a "such" something, whereas proper names are supposed to name a substance, a "this" something.

In reading the works of ancient philosophers one may notice the close connection (if not confusion) on the one hand between the categories of common-proper names, and on the other hand between the categories of universal-particulars or substances. In the works of Aristotle, for example, one may observe such connections. In *Prior Analytic* a distinction is made between two kinds of expressions i.e., those which denote only a unique entity and those that are predicated of kinds of entities. "Of all things which exist some are such that they cannot be predicated of anything else truly and universally, e.g. Cleon and Callias, i.e. the individual and sensible, but other things may be predicated of them (for each of these is both man and animal) ... for as a rule each sensible thing is such that it cannot be predicated of anything save incidentally: for we sometimes say that that white object is Socrates, or that that which approaches is Callias." (B.I.: ch. I. 27).

In a similar vein Plato was concerned with names, both proper and common, even though in his dialogues one cannot find a clear distinction between these two categories. Proper names both denote uniquely the individual and at the same time function as a predicate characterizing the individual (*Theaetetus*. 209).

However in one dialogue, i.e. *Cratylus*, Plato almost solves the general problem concerning names and the particular problem of proper names.

The problem in this dialogue is the relation between language and the world. Socrates rejects both the realistic and the nominalistic theories of language represented respectively by Cratylus and Hermogenes in favour of another theory which we called Instrumentalism (see, *Universals: A new look at an old Problem*).

Socrates refutes on various grounds the alternatives either *Phuiss* (nature) or *Nomos* (convention), that either words are dictated by the nature of things or are imposed arbitrarily upon things. The significant part of the dialogue, however is the Socratic discovery of a way-out of the dilemma.

To appreciate the full force of the Socratic insight I will quote part of the discussion between Socrates and Hermogens:

Soc. And speech is a kind of action?

Her. True.

Soc. And will a man speak correctly who speaks as he pleases? Will not a successful speaker rather be he who speaks in the natural way of speaking, and as things ought to spoken and with the natural instrument? Any other mode of speaking will result in error and failure.

Her. I quite agree with you.

Soc. And is not naming a part of speaking? For in giving names men speak.

Her. That is true.

Soc. And if speaking is a sort of action and has a relation to acts, is not naming also a sort of action?

.

.

.

.

.

.

Soc. Very good: then a name is an instrument?

Her. Certainly.

Soc. And now suppose that I ask a similar question about names. Will you answer me? Regarding the name as an instrument, what do we do when we name?

Her. I cannot say.

Soc. Do we not give information to one another, and distinguish things according to their nature?

Her. Certainly we do. (388)

In this work I made use of four Socratic contentions which are compressed in the quoted portion i.e., that (1) *Speech* is a kind of action, (2) to speak successfully and felicitously one should observe a certain convention, (3) naming is a sort of action, and (4) the name is an instrument used by speaker to convey information and to distinguish entities.

Throughout my concern was to provide an answer to the question; What is in a Name? To answer this question we examined in some detail various views of recent philosophers, contemporary logicians, and linguists. We observed that though there were some germs of truth here and there in these theories, none were adequate to the facts of language.

On the constructive side we made the following observations:

Proper names encompass various classes such as Personal Names, Place Names, Times Names, Institution Names and Artifact Names. The paradigm of names is of course Personal Name which are classified into First-Middle-Sur-Names, Patronym, Cognomen, Mythical Names, Fictitious Names, etc.

We observed that the common denomenator of these categories is their pragmatic property of being used for certain ends – and not their purported semantic property of denoting spatio-

temporal objects or syntactic property of being replacable by
definite descriptions or their grammatical structures.

We observed that proper names, like singular demonstrative
pronouns, singular personal and impersonal pronouns, and definite descriptions, are used as Referring Expressions.

We observed however, that unlike pronouns which are used by
different speakers to denote different entities on different occasions of their use, proper names, like definite descriptions, are
always *purported* in any particular context to name one and only
one entity. Since a proper name is used for referring to an entity
for individuating it, it should always be applied to the same
entity, though the same entity may have various names.

We next made a distinction between proper names and definite
description by noting that there are things which are true of
proper names and false of definite descriptions.

A name, however, may be used as a description, and being used
in this manner loses its function of uniquely individuating an
entity.

We noted that a proper name may be assimilated into a
common-name if in virtue of association with its bearer absorbs
some of its properties.

Nonetheless one must always distinguish (A) the meaning of
proper name, i.e., the constant and salient feature which may be
described as a property of being used to make a unique reference
to the same entity and thereby to individuate the bearer so that
it could be amenable to description, evaluation, registration,
nomination etc., (B) the bearer of the name, which could exist in
various ontological domains, (C) the unique properties of the
bearer, and (D) the connotation of a name, i.e., the accidental
feature of association of a name with its bearer which the hearer
may make upon hearing that name. Finally we discussed various
but subsidiary issues connected with the use of proper names
such as the protean functions of names, transformation into
common names, *ad hoc* conventions pertaining to names, problems of translation of names, etc.

I assumed throughout that the best method of finding a
plausible answer to the various problems of meaning, sense,
denotation, and connotation of names is to observe how certain
kinds of expressions called proper names are actually used in

various situations and how their functions differ from the behavior of other types of linguistic expressions.

Now if these observations enable an inquirer to render intelligible why something is a proper name and help him to classify a certain unfamiliar sound as a name, then here is a theory for explaining the old puzzle.

BIBLIOGRAPHY

Ayer, A., "Names and Descriptions," *The Concept of a Person*, St. Martin's Press, 1963.

Chomsky, N., *Aspects of the Theory of Syntax*, The M.I.T. Press, 1965.

Church, A., *Introduction to Mathematical Logic*, Vol. 1, Princeton, 1959.

Frege, G., *The Foundations of Arithmetic*, translated by J. L. Austin, Basil Blackwell, 1950.

— "On Sense and Nominatum," *Readings in Philosophical Analysis*, eds. Feigl and Sellars, Appleton-Century, 1949.

Gardiner, A., *The Theory of Speech and Language*, Oxford. Clarendon., 1932.

— *The Theory of Proper Names: A Controversial Essay*. London; Oxford Press, 1954.

Green, L., *Law of Names*, New York: Oceana Publications, 1954.

Jespersen, O., *The Philosophy of Grammar*, London: Allen and Unwin, 1924.

— *Essentials of English Grammar*, London: George Allen, 1960.

Katz, J., "Review of Semantic Analysis," *Language*, Vol. 38, No. 1.

Kneale, W. and M., *The Development of Logic*, Oxford: Clarendon Press, 1962.

Linsky, L., *Referring*, Routledge and Kegan Paul, London, 1967.

Mathews, C., *English Surnames*, London: Weidenfeld and Nicholson, 1966.

Mill, J., *A System of Logic*, 10th ed., London: Longmans Green and Co., 1879.

Patridge, E., *Name into Word: Proper Names That Have Become Common Property*, New York: Macmillan, 1950.

Quine, W., *Methods of Logic*, New York: Holt-Dryden, 1960.

Russell, B., *Introduction to Mathematical Philosophy*, London, 1919.

— *An Inquiry into Meaning and Truth*, London: George Allen, 1940.

— "Proper Names," *Human Knowledge*, New York, Simon and Schusler, 1948.

— "The Philosophy of Logical Atomism," *Logic and Knowledge*, ed. R. C. Marsh, London: Allen and Unwin, 1951.

Searle, J., "Proper Names," *Mind*, LXVII, No. 261, 1958.

— "Proper Names and Descriptions," *The Encyclopedia of Philosophy*, Vol. 6, New York: Collier-Macmillan, 1967.

Shawyder, D., *Modes of Referring and the Problem of Universals*, University of California Press, 1961.

— "Review of the Meaning of Proper Names by H. S. Sørensen," *The Journal of Philosophy*, LXI, No. 15, 1964.

Sørensen, H., *The Meaning of Proper Names: With a Definiens Formula for Proper Names in Modern English*, Copenhagen: Gad Publishers, 1963.

— *Word-Classes in Modern English*, Copenhagen: Gad Publishers, 1958.

Strawson, P., "On Referring," *Philosophy and Ordinary Language*, ed. C. G. Caton, University of Illinois Press, 1963.

— *Introduction to Logical Theory*, London: Methuen, 1952.

— "Review of Wittgenstein's Philosophical Investigations," *Mind*, Vol. LXIII, 1954.

— *Individual*, London: Methuen, 1959.

— "Review of Sørensen 'The Meaning of Proper Names' ", *Mind*, Vol. LXXV, 1966.

Witycombe, E., *The Oxford Dictionary of English Christian Names*, London: Oxford Press, 1947.

Wittgenstein, L., *Philosophical Investigations*, translated by G. E. M. Anscombe, Oxford: Basil Blackwell, 1954.

Zabeeh, F., *Universals: A New Look at an Old Problem*, The Hague: Martinus Nijhoff, 1966.

Ziff, P., *Semantic Analysis*, New York: Cornell University Press, 1960.

INDEX

The manufacturer's authorised representative in the EU is Springer
Nature Customer Service Centre GmbH, Europaplatz 3, 69115 Heidelberg,
Germany. If you have any concerns regarding our products, please
contact ProductSafety@springernature.com

Printed and bound by CPI Group (UK) Ltd, Croydon, CR0 4YY

29/04/2026

02099458-0014